MOB JUSTICE

MOB JUSTICE

ANJU KHOSLA

2009

SBS Publishers & Distributors Pvt. Ltd.
New Delhi

ISBN : 9788189741860

First Published in India in 2009

Printed in India

Published by:-

SBS Publishers & Distributors Pvt. Ltd.,
2/9, Ground Floor, Ansari Road,
Darya Ganj, New Delhi -110002,
India.

Tel:- 0091.11.23289119 / 32945311 / 41563911
Email:- mail@sbspublishers.com
www.sbspublishers.com

Printed at
SYNDICATE BINDERS
A-20, Hosiery Complex, Phase-II,
Noida - 201305

Preface

Every criminal is entitled to due process of the law and this fact forms the cornerstone of any civilized judicial system. In India there is a spate of lynching in recent times. How do we interpret this new form of justice system in present context? Have the people lost their faith in the police completely to indulge in such wanton acts of vigilante justice? Or is it that under particular regime tenure, people become more confident and daring!

'All that is required for evil to triumph,' wrote British parliamentarian Edmund Burke, some 300 years ago, 'is for good men to do nothing' Efforts ought to be undertaken by those in higher echelons of power to curb the growing tendency among seemingly law-abiding citizens to bypass the institutions established by law for the speedy re-dressal of grievances.

Daredevil acts are done by the crowd on behalf of the *local* community. Mob psychology shows that individuals tend to behave in a different manner as part of a group in contrast to acting independently. Individuals in a group defer their goals and take upon the identity of the group. Therefore, members of a group are likely to commit acts they would never commit alone. Being in a group allows individuals to defer blame, responsibility, accountability, and/or judgment upon the group.

An incident of mob justice, in addition to being a shocking indicator of the psychological mindset of a society, also suggests a failed justice delivery mechanism. If instant justice is meted out to an offender then is the punishment just in degree for a crime? Anybody who is alleged to have committed a crime must be given the opportunity to defend himself or herself. The situation about instant justice is unacceptable especially under a constitutional rule, because the laws are clear about taking people through the criminal justice system where alleged people should be take to court and proper punishment meeted out to them.

Some feel that the police protection is not adequate and are not efficient enough! The police needs to be quick and brisk in action, as people get frustrated seeing criminals free on the street after sending them to the police station, and this motivates people to beat up alleged thieves.

Humans use threats and violence to dominate, and also resort to cheating, deceit or negotiation to obtain status and valued resources. Moreover impulsive violent behaviours are frequently labeled emotional violence and are linked with emotions such as anger and fear. The common man the politician, the police, the judiciary and the media if work together the barbaric tradition of mob justice in modern times can be nipped in the bud.

Anju Khosla

Contents

Chatpter 1

Introduction

A nation has police institutions and the legal system [under which] which people are punished accordingly.

The situation about instant justice is unacceptable especially under a constitutional rule, because the laws of most countries are clear about taking people through the criminal justice system where alleged people should be take to court and proper punishment meeted out to them.

Most people join mob action because they have been victims of such incidents.

Mob justice, is "barbaric." It reverses us to the animal kingdom where hooliganism and cannibalism take place.

Anyone accused of a crime that seriously hurts or kills someone is often considered to be guilty and deserving of the most extreme punishment.

Mob justice has been with us too long, but due to limited media coverage in the past, it could not easily be heard. But thanks to the proliferation of the media now, mob justice cases can now easily be heard. Though there are no provisions for the offence called instant justice in the criminal code, putting a person to death without trial is a crime.

Mob is when a large angry mob takes justice into their own hands. Usually ends with somebody getting hanged, torched or pitchfork'd. A common method of dispensing justice in the more rural areas of a country.

Angry mob is a large congregation of people banding together to take down whatever it is they think is plaguing their life. They usually carry torches and pitch forks

Lynch is any sort of extralegal justice that involves a mob killing someone in an unusually painful or public way.

large group of people attack a single person or a small group of people, usually innocent and unsuspecting, and beating him/them, sometimes to death, in a very violent and barbaric manner by *attacked with slapping, punching, kicking, and spitting.*

Lynch is a cowardly and disrespectful action, as the victim has no option of defending himself against the attackers, because they highly outnumber him.

the hanging is not the bad part the torture comes first lynching comes from slavery when slave owners had problems with their slaves they would call a man i forgot his first name but his last name waz lynch and he would com and show them how to torture their slaves but not kill them so they would not disrespect their owners.

Self Experience

Frustrated by the inability of the police to respond adequately to their (Nigeria) safety and security needs, citizens have resorted to self-help measures. The most controversial of these is the formation of militant vigilante groups—some of which have made lynching and torturing criminal suspects their stock in trade.

Countries like Nigeria and South Africa have prominent vigilante groups who hand out punishment to suspected criminals. How is your community dealing with crime?

Public opinion of vigilante groups is divided. A part of the public argues that vigilante activities should be regulated and closely supervised by the national police. Another part calls for outright disbandment of vigilante groups and trial of their operatives, who take delight in judging potential offenders without trial and in administering brutal punishment—and who are undermining our progress toward democracy.

Human rights groups and policymakers must find a way to ensure both that due process is protected and that the rights of communities to organize and protect themselves are respected. The first step is to differentiate between vigilante groups that employ "mob justice" in their operations—whose modus operandi cannot be tolerated in a democratic society and which should be disbanded—and those whose activities are amenable to the rule of law and due process and that could work (and do work) under close police supervision. Many groups that promote racial discrimination, religious persecution, and state-sponsored violence operate under the guise of vigilantism. These groups not only offend sensibilities, but also violate every human rights treaty that Nigeria has ratified.

Reporting

Have been a victim of mob violence when I stole money so that I could buy hashish. I was mobbed and almost died in hospital. The experience was good because I stopped stealing as I knew the next time I might be killed.

Fuad, Nairobi, Kenya

Mob justice has been a part of Ghanaian culture since before I was born. I have personally witnessed several instances where taxi drivers have parked their cabs, passengers and all, in order to join a mob action which they have no clue about. On one such occasion, an alleged thief managed to escape the original group chasing him. He then pointed at somebody else shouting "dzulo, dzulo" - "thief, thief". Within a few minutes, this innocent man was besieged by an angry mob but thankfully the police were quick to respond and saved his life.

Sheriff, London, UK

Having seen mob justice first hand on a trip to Nigeria, I can honestly say I think it is awful and too easy for innocent people to become victims. On a cross country journey, our bus was attacked by a crowd of about 100 men.The windows were smashed, the tyres were slashed and we were threatened with being set on fire. What was the crime? Apparently, a driver who worked for the same bus company had knocked down and killed an 'area boy' in that village the day before. The driver of our bus, (who was no doubt not the driver from the previous day), was dragged from our bus and beaten. I dread to think what happened to him. I can honestly say I have never been so terrified in my life.

Rachael, UK

I agree that we need to reform our legal and security systems in Africa. Mob justice is barbaric; it is living and relating like senseless animals. God will hold everyone responsible who takes the law into his/her hands to kill a fellow human being.

Osarumwense, Aba, Nigeria

Living in Tanzania, I come across mob justice all the time. Mostly the accused have done wrong, but there are those other times when they are innocent and have no way of proving it. Recently beneath my house, three civilians and one security guard were caught trying to steal. They were beaten up right in front of our eyes by the police. Next day in our local news paper it was said that the mob was responsible. I am totally against mob justice, but first you have to stop the police participation. Only then will the public stop theirs.

Anonymous, Tanzania

One day in Monrovia's most crowded market place called Waterside, a teenager ran into a woman who suspected the lad was attempting to snatch her bag. Instead of calling the police she yelled "rogue! rogue!" – an alarm which invites irate crowds to discipline pickpockets. A crowd had no sooner begun to throw blows at the poor fellow, than a team of policemen arrived and rescued him. On scrutiny, the boy who was now bleeding turned out to be half-blind – much to the horror of everybody around. He had run into the woman simply due to his poor sight. This case is a serious indictment of mob justice. Such jungle justice can't be anything worth the word deterrence; it simply gives sadists a feed day in the marketplace. It shouldn't be condoned.

Martin Toe, Liberia, Washington DC, USA

The common man has become so desperate in his bid to survive that anyone who touches his daily bread is in trouble. I am sure that if these people didn't have to worry about their basic necessities, they would not dish out immediate justice. But this desperation should not be seen as an excuse to continue jungle justice. It is wrong, no matter how hungry we get. If we forget our values, we will be reduced to nothing. There is no way that mob justice can be condoned.

P.M. Lagos

Mob justice is not correct or fair, but it is effective and efficient. Let people work for their living and not steal, otherwise the mob is the only solution.

Momodou Sanneh, UK/Gambia

Why do we assume that mob justice only happens in countries like Nigeria, South Africa *et al*? The reaction to the Rodney King verdict in Los Angeles, USA was a classic case of mob justice.

Bola, New York City, USA

Anyone supporting mob justice has not seen all its permutations. If they do, they will not support it all. The one example I saw left my brain numb, and I don't think I have been the same person since. After the civil war in Nigeria, many people became very distrustful of others. In Kaduna, I saw a man burnt to death because he took a loaf of bread from his son, broke it, and gave the other half to a small girl crying for her mother to give her bread. The mother got offended and shouted that the man was trying to kidnap her daughter. The man was burnt to death because local soldiers only heard too late to do anything about it. Mob justice is not justice; I will not stand for it.

Che Sunday, San Francisco, USA

The "eye for an eye" mentality will, as Martin Luther King said, leaves the world blind.

Rudi Muller, Vancouver, Canada

When I was young in Aba, eastern Nigeria, I saw a man lynched and set ablaze for allegedly picking another man's pocket. After the man had been set on fire, someone demanded to know what exactly the man had stolen. Nobody in the crowd could say. Such killings are everywhere because the majority of people do not believe in our judicial system. The general feeling is that the accused person could walk free if handed over to the police, and people argue that mob justice discourages people from stealing and so saves the authorities the time and money of prosecution.

Chinedu Ibeabuchi, Lagos, Nigeria

I suppose if someone posed a real threat to me or my family - I'm talking about a kill or be killed situation here - then I could take the law into my hands. I don't think most people see mob justice as a first resort. But sometimes it seems like the only way for those whose justice systems have failed them.

Ngum Ngafor, Manchester, UK

I have been working in Tanzania for nearly seven months and have witnessed several mob actions. It really is not pleasant to see, but I believe it keeps the crime rate down. The corruption within the police in Tanzania is unbelievable and I have heard about cases where people have to pay the police before they even investigate. I come from South Africa where we live in fear: The courts are backlogged with cases and the justice process is extremely slow. If the vigilante groups can sort out criminals, I can live with that.

Paul Sands, Dar es Salaam, Tanzania

Due to corruption in our judiciary and police forces, criminals can sometime "buy" their freedom and society is left with no option but to take the law into its own hands. But this itself is a crime which should be condemned: two wrongs will never make a right.

Kisanya Vincent, Nairobi, Kenya

The problem we have in Africa is a lack of proper investigation before taking action. For example, sometimes in southern Nigeria, somebody will go to the vigilantes to report an enemy as a thief because they want revenge. The vigilante then goes straight to the person and punishes them. I think we need proper training on how to investigate crimes before action is taken.

John, Nigeria

Mob justice is not the answer to stealing. I believe that if our law enforcement officers would go the extra mile in fighting crime, then this can stop. A lot of people get upset and end up taking the law into their own hands because police officers drag their feet in combating crime.

Onthatile B.B. Maswibilili, Malaysia/Botswana

When the people lose confidence in the security apparatus of the state, what else do you expect? When a neighbourhood thief is released so quickly from the police station that you get home to meet him chatting with friends, what next?

Nana Biney, Ghana

Mob justice is not justice at all. It is a feud between individuals that gains intensity as others vent their anger in the heat of the moment. It is easy to get caught up in the thrill of things and a mob can be a very appealing way to let off steam. Instead, one should think before jumping in and throwing fists. A few punches will release some steam, but the dissatisfaction with life will return when things settle down.

Keturah, USA

People take the law into their hands because the justice system has failed them. When you take a thief to the police station, you hardly reach your house again before the thief is set free by the police who have collected a fee from him. Most people in my town in Cameroon have resorted to mob justice because they are frustrated. This has reduced crime a bit. Although mistaken identity may result in the death of someone innocent, most of the time the mob is right and this is actually yielding fruits.

Teneng Lucas Chefor, Cameroon

It is a terrible thing for a mob to take the law into their hands. A lot of mistakes are made and innocent people are often victimised. There should be massive public awareness programmes to educate the people on the risks of mob violence. Today it might be a stranger, tomorrow it may be you or somebody close to you.

Charles Udekwe, USA

Mob justice is never the answer, but with an unreliable police force it becomes an alternative to discourage would-be criminals. Sometimes people have to take the law into their own hands to protect the interests of the community. Let the law enforcement officers do a good job and then there would be no room for mob justice.

Matongo Maumbi, Chikuni, Monze, Zambia!

A distinction must be made between mob justice and other alternative justice systems in Africa. Most vigilante systems are quite different from an irate mob dealing spontaneously with a criminal who has been caught red-handed in a crowded area like the marketplace. Vigilante systems are more like security outfits organised by members of a community to actively police their neighbourhood. Plus it is worth pointing out that no country has a perfect system; they are continually being improved.

Sonny, Lagos, Nigeria

Mob justice might deter 'little' thieves in countries like mine, Nigeria, but I believe it should be stopped since it doesn't work on the big-bellied, rich organised criminals who have the best security officials.

Okafor David, USA/Nigeria

Mob justice is not good. It has never resolved anything. I have come to interpret mob justice as a pathway to revenge. I have talked to participants in mob action and they told me that all they wanted was to vent their anger. Mob justice is a result of the failure of law enforcement agencies and governments to justly prosecute those who commit criminal acts against the weak in the society. When the law starts to protect the 'higher-ups' and people with connections to government, then mob justice becomes the only way out for the downtrodden.

E. Julu Swen, Monrovia, Liberia

Common people are worst affected when the justice system doesn't work. In Dar es Salaam where I live and work, mob lynching is no longer news to most of us, especially those living in highly populated areas. Such areas are home to a massive number of unemployed youths some of whom turn to criminal activities like petty theft. Losing a thousand shillings (less than one pound sterling) through theft may not sound much to someone living in a posh area, but it may mean a whole family missing out on their dinner in a poorer area. Should we be surprised if such victims participate in mob lynching?

Wesley Nsomba, Dar es Salaam, Tanzania

The abolition of the death penalty for capital offenders in South Africa and the unreliable judicial systems in most African countries can be very frustrating. People, therefore, resort to mob action which is aptly termed "jungle justice" in Nigeria. Although crude, it serves a very useful purpose in discouraging criminals in certain areas like Ajegunle in Lagos, Nigeria.

Ohagwam Franklyn, Johannesburg, South Africa.

Mob justice is simply the easiest and fastest way of choosing jurors to serve justice. When government fails, do you expect the people to sit and watch?

Blessing Young, America

I really love the topic of mob justice as I feel it is apt. I am in an internet cafe at the moment writing to you and a gunshot rang out not too long ago. Reason: factions of a local vigilante group are at each other's throats. Some of these groups engage in extra-judiciary killings which are exceedingly abhorrent. But these events raise pertinent questions. What is it in our law-enforcement arrangement that makes citizens reluctant to hand criminals over to the police? And doesn't this penchant for mob justice show that people have lost trust in judges?

I. Chukwudi. Lagos, Nigeria

In most cases, what we call jungle justice, that is dealing with a thief on the spot, serves as a deterrent. When such a thief is handed over to police they may later release him or her due to a lack of proper evidence. But, I have seen cases where innocent citizens have been killed due to mistaken identity. The only means of correcting it is for the government to reform our justice system.

Eleso Sunday, Abuja, Nigeria

The practice of mob justice should be discouraged because it can lead to the killing of innocent people. Anyone who practices such evil acts should be prosecuted.

Peter Tuach, Minnesota, USA

What alternatives do the masses have when the police fail to protect them and the judicial system fails to put criminals behind bars? No one seems to care about the common people on the street. Mob justice is not the answer; it is a symptom of what is wrong in Africa. We need serious reforms.

Stephen Gitau, Kenyan, USA

Mob justice is sadly inadequate because it lacks the careful examination and deliberation required to discover the truth and respond with appropriate action. Mobs are driven by strong emotions and reason is abandoned. Mobs can get the wrong people and they mete out a "justice" that is usually far more violent than the crime. Even in countries where the justice system is inadequate, mob "justice" is usually just another face of crime: it is lawless, violent, cruel, and arbitrary.

Clint, Los Angeles, USA

In all cases mob justice is not justice at all but a mass crime. Those that carry out the 'mob justice' have neither investigative ability nor intention to investigate. The victim has no opportunity to defend themselves and even when caught red-handed, the execution style punishment does not fit the crime. This in some cases can be regarded as gang violence. This is the result of the lack of trust in the government security system. What a shame!

Greg, Cameroon & USA

When justice is not transparent, then the mob comes in. This is not only in Africa but around the world.

Henry Williams, New York/Sierra Leone

"As human beings sometimes it is difficult to identify two people, of which one may be a thief and the other innocent, so if anybody who is believed to have stolen the fellow must be handed over to the police to also conduct investigations leading to the prosecution of the alleged thief.

On the other hand if the thief is caught red handed and he is beaten that is okay to serve as a deterrent to other thieves.

Cecelia Gyewu, 42, Official Town

The police are not efficient enough because I quite remember there was a day that someone was lynched almost to death around the Ga-Mantse Palace. [Someone] called the police but they did not respond to the call; the body which was lying naked was at the scene till the evening.

Charles Kofi Joe Dogbatse, 26, North Kaneshie

I once experienced a situation where I called the police and they told me that I should mobilise people to arrest the fellow and bring him to the police station. The police must act according to their responsibility on paper."

Ras Liberty, 29, Alajo

LYCHING HISTORY OF THE WEST

In the 19th century, lynching had been used in the Midwest and West as a means of meting out quick justice when jails and courtrooms were few. But after the Civil War, whites in the defeated South, who blamed African-Americans for their troubles and focused their hatred on the supposed threat of black men to white women, made lynchings into festivals of racial intimidation.

Often, the victims were suspected of having committed a serious crime. But it didn't take a crime to spark a lynching. Blacks were lynched for failing to step aside on a sidewalk, or accidentally brushing against a white woman. Even when a crime had been committed, lynch mobs often didn't wait for a suspect to be arrested, much less convicted. Instead, the mob played the role of judge, jury, and executioner. In fact, in cases when a suspect had been arrested, mobs often had to break into jail and kidnap the prisoner in order to kill him or her.

Lynch squads often included a town's prominent citizens: bankers, lawyers, merchants, and legislators. The police and the courts looked the other way. When a jailbreak was involved, it often happened with a wink from the sheriff. Rarely was anyone ever arrested for lynching. Until 1930, only four people were ever sent to jail for it.

Many lynchings took place in a carnival atmosphere. Sometimes newspapers announced the event in advance. People came from miles around, occasionally riding special excursion trains chartered for the spectacle. Children were often among the onlookers, and schools delayed their classes until they returned. Witnesses collected souvenirs from the victims, including bits of clothing, hair, and bones.

Lynching was part of a prevalent attitude of racial discrimination. Without Sanctuary quotes a black Mississippian's recollection of the 1930s:

> Back in those days, to kill a Negro wasn't nothing. It was like killing a chicken or killing a snake. The whites would say, `Niggers jest supposed to die, ain't no damn good anyway—so jest go on an' kill `em'.

A Little Rock, Arkansas, newspaper saw lynching as a helpful part of a system of racial control, curbing the danger that black men might get out of line and cast their "lustful eyes on white women":

> This my be `Southern brutality' as far as the Boston Negro can see, but in polite circles, we call it Southern chivalry, a Southern virtue that will never die.

But less than one quarter of lynching victims were even accused of attacking white women.

Today, thanks to civil rights laws, changing attitudes, and better law enforcement, racial killing as a community festival has passed from the scene. There were disturbing echoes of the age of lynching in June 1998, when three avowed racists chained James Byrd Jr., an African-American, to a pickup truck and dragged him to his death near Jasper, Texas. But in this case, the three killers were convicted—two condemned to die, one sentenced to life imprisonment

Police Successes

Five suspects will appear in the Brakpan Magistrates' Court on Monday, 30 April 2007 to answer on four charges of murder each. They have been arrested in connection with the mob-killing on Sunday 15 April 2007. Four men suspected of being responsible for burglaries in the Langaville area were beaten to death during that attack.

Detectives from the Tsakane police station diligently followed up on every piece of information they could possibly obtain. This led to the identification and arrest of three women and two men during the early hours of this morning (26 April 2007). They are between the ages of 37 and 55-years. All of them reside in Langaville Ext 8.

The police wishes to seriously warn the public not to take the law into their own hands. All incidents of mob justice or vigilantism will always be vigorously investigated. Those responsible for any violence committed during such actions will be arrested and they will be held accountable for their actions in a court of law.

SITUATION IN INDIA

The Past

Mob vigilantes are not new in India or the world at large. In India, it dates back to the days of *Tenali Ram* and *Birbal*, when those who dared to step on the wrong side of the law were paraded in streets in various stages of undress, either riding backwards on asses, or being dragged behind one. With their faces blackened, they were booed publicly, stoned, and humiliated using any means possible. Public shaming in those times enjoyed regal sanction.

Victims were often scarred for life, physically and emotionally; but the justification that they brought it upon themselves often ignored issues of justice. For instance, did an accused deserve to be mauled publicly before his or her crime had been proved? But since the justification provided by vigilante groups was ineffective governance and law enforcement, very often extreme brutality and sadism was par for the course.

Vigilantes have, after all, had very positive connotations too in popular stories, such as Robinhood, and comic books. Batman, Spiderman, Superman were pure vigilantes with the public's interests at heart. Perhaps, that is why a lot of vigilantes convince themselves that their motivations are pure even when they act on prejudices. Heck, even the Klu Klux Klan probably feels morally justified in carrying out its vicious executions and violence. For that matter, all the genocides and riots that have happened in history have been carried out by those who fancy themselves to be vigilantes fighting for truth and justice.

Not much seems to have changed since those times. What we see today could merely be revival of a tradition long buried under the anglicized annals of penal codes and archives of dusty, musty case studies. What has perhaps changed is the role media has played in popularizing our vigilante force.

A Thorny Issue

Mob justice is always a thorny issue and most of the time; it can prove to be counter-productive. This occurs when a section of the society assumes the role of a vigilante for correcting a social wrong specially the use of vigilante justice when a section of population runs out of all other feasible options. Such justice deliverance methods often arouse passions among people although they may be discounted as infeasible or even illegal.

The matter has now taken a communal colour, because our opportunity hungry politicians can never let a chance like this slip.

The frustration of a section of the population towards state corruption and soaring crime leads to this type of behaviour. More situations include where the people, neighbors, communities, fed up with police and other agencies who fail to carry out their duties to society, will handle things more and more themselves. They'll take it upon themselves to organize and improve their communities themselves, because they will finally admit that the institutions aren't going to do it for them. This will start happening more and more, clashes with official authority.

In bustling Bhagalpur town in India, a mob nearly beat to death a man who was accused of snatching a gold chain from a woman.

What was more shocking was the fact that the incident took place in the presence of two policemen, one of the police officer also participated by dragging the suspect around by his legs tied to the officer's motor-cycle? All this was filmed by a local news channel. Other horrific case of public lynching and beatings includes three suspected motorcycle thieves were caught by villagers in Nawada district and brutally beaten up with sticks, stones and metal rods. The enraged mob even gouged out an eye of one of the suspects, Tinku Singh, with a pointed iron tool. The three men were taken to hospital. Then, two men caught stealing material at a thermal power station in Begusarai district was beaten up by locals in the presence of policemen. In Nawada district, two children, aged 13 and 12 years, were beaten up by locals and paraded with their heads shaved for allegedly stealing salt and detergents from a local grocery where they were employed. Such mob anger is not restricted to the villages alone.

On August 30, 2007 the Maoists killed 12 policemen in Chhattisgarh state. Bodies of three police officers killed in the incident were recovered with their eyes gouged off. The killing of 12 police officers was the latest incident in the ongoing triangular conflict in that state between the state police, a state sponsored private militiatry the Salwa Judum, and the Maoists.

On March 26 2008 In yet another case of mob violence, a man from a dalit family was beaten to death in a Bihar town, the police said Wednesday.

The victim, Bharat Dom, was beaten to death in Daulatganj are of Chapra town Tuesday, according to the police.

The police said a mob caught the man in his mid-40s on suspicion of having stolen a cow from the house of Amarnath Pandey.

'He was beaten to death with bricks and bamboo sticks,' the police said. "A murder case has been lodged, but no suspect has been identified."

The incident comes a day after an elderly man was reportedly lynched in a village in Bihar's Munger district when he intervened to save his grandson in a dispute over a love affair. The police have arrested three accused in this case.

In the last two and a half months, nearly a dozen cases of lynching have been reported across the state.

In rural Bihar, 'mob justice' is common. Last year, over three dozen similar incidents were reported and many more may have gone unnoticed.

The worst lynching case was reported in September last year when 10 men from the underprivileged Kueri community were beaten to death in Vaishali district on suspicion that they were thieves. Later, a high-level probe found that the men were innocent.

These incidents, shows contrasting pictures, are the latest in the ongoing internal turmoil in India. Violence committed against the state agencies, particularly against the local police, and those committed by mobs against suspects of crime are not isolated incidents in India, though the extent of brutality as depicted in the above incidents are rare.

Increasing incidences of mob justice can be linked to state's failure to address legitimate grievances along with the inherently violent nature of the Indian society.

Villagers Greviences and Protection of the Citizenry

Villagers complaint, quite rightly as it turns out that despite increased incidences of thefts and repeated complaints, the police had taken no action. Frustrated, the villagers took the law into their own hands. Where there are people, there are cliques. Where there are cliques, there are rumours, and so on and so forth.

While the frustration of the villagers at the failure of the state to punish lawbreakers is understandable, lynching ten people for stealing points to a deeper malaise than merely police inaction What is more worrisome is that the trigger point for violent outrages seems to be constantly lowering from violent crimes like Dacoity, armed burglary e.t.c to merely stealing. While it won't be fair to draw such conclusions based on sketchy data, it won't be entirely presumptuous to conclude that the villagers' primary purpose was to kill.

The state urgently needs to revamp the governance structure. But that is not enough. It must move against the perpetrators of mob justice and punish them severely. Admittedly, the state has lost its moral authority by its failure to discharge its most basic function: protection of the citizenry.

Till action is taken against mobs even in cases where their action may seem "justified", the state would have no incentive to improve governance. State failure is almost guaranteed in two cases:

- First, when it usurps the function of the market and the civil society.
- Second, when it allows its own basic function to be taken over by non-state actors. Private justice should be an anathema in a constitutional democracy.

Vigilante Justice or 'Street Justice'

An army of plainclothes superheroes is out on a rampage at the next corner. These self-styled superheroes, who hunt in packs, don't wait for court trials.

They are the new face of India's punishment paratroopers, who leave no stone unturned in doling out retribution against petty criminals, traitors to morality, or simply those stung by the news channels' apian reporters.

In rural Bihar, 'street justice' is becoming increasingly common. Last year, over three dozen cases of lynching were reported and many more have gone unreported.

The worst lynching case was reported in September last year when 10 people from the underprivileged Kueri community in Vaishali district were beaten to death over an alleged theft. Later, a high-level probe found that the men were not thieves as the villagers had suspected.

vigilante action is reminiscent of odd bits of news we heard when a certain Panchayat of a certain village, flouting all form of civility, created a parallel court of justice. Punishment by the village folk could range anywhere from parading women in the nude for alleged debauchery, or outright killing of the accused for 'crimes' such as falling in love with someone of another caste. The phenomenon seems to have spread out of the rural backdrop.

The urban is no longer urbane as the country's great rural-urban divide appears fuzzy. With people from rural areas migrating to larger towns and cities, the mob culture comes naturally as an add-on.

What is interesting is how it has inspired more urban folk to join in, for their share of the penalty pie. What is even more interesting is the stance the vigilante adopts on what it considers as public outrage, and the means it adopts to mete justice. The same crowd, while beating its King Kong chest over rapists, adulterers, prostitutes, and anything 'amoral', does not think twice when delivering punishment. The defaulters in the eyes of the vigilante are, more often than not, deprived of any vestments, and paraded nude or semi-nude as part of the process. Opportunistic voyeurism, in the very least? Or a reflection on the repressed angst that finds a vent at times like this? Take your pick. Meanwhile, the vigilante will carry on rapping the rapist, and raping all norms of reason.

Point of Collapse

The rising incidence of vigilante justice, lynching and public humiliation of petty criminals across the country by angry mobs is further evidence that public confidence in the law, order and justice systems is on the point of collapse.

In the past few years incidents of violence committed in the name of 'justice' are increasingly reported from India. These are acts of violence, is resorted to by either the state agents or the people for executing what they think is justice. Such violence indicates that the public perception of justice in India is rapidly changing and changing for the worse.

The people's perception of justice depends upon how the justice dispensation mechanism in a country functions. In theory, India has a reasonably good legislative framework within which laws are drafted, debated and implemented. But in practice the drafting and debating of laws remain mostly outside the scope of any public discourse. The acts of the legislature are often dominated by caste, religious and partisan political sentiments as opposed to welfare and betterment of the people.

Mob justice is not an exclusive phenomenon attributed to Bihar, however, although it is reported in alarming numbers from that state. Victims in some 25 cases in the past 12 months, in fact, were killed. Mob justice is a common phenomenon across the country in which a suspect, if caught by the local populace, is often "softened" before being handed to the police. The police further torture the person to extract a confession, and the entire investigation of the case is based upon this forced confession. Cases brought to court based on evidence gathered following a forced confession by torture stand little chance of succeeding during a trial, and thus, the result is an acquittal of the accused. Given to the type of socio-economic conditions in India; the chance of an acquitted person being caught while committing yet another crime is very high. Additionally, there is an enormous delay, often for periods of six to seven years or even a decade, for the courts to complete a trial.

The net result is the loss of the perception of justice in the mind of the public. Consequently, in this context, it is natural at this juncture for the public to take the law into their own hands and render instant justice upon anyone whom they suspect of a crime.

Social scientist Shaibal Gupta does not agree.

"This only reveals the state of Bihar. People think justice will not be delivered. So they resort to instant justice by lynching the culprit," he says. The alternative to mob justice is elite justice, and what we have to do is strike a balance.

Must people resort to barbaric and uncivilized mob or jungle justice tactics to fight crime in 21st century? Mob justice is only a slightly more sophisticated form of jungle justice. Jungle justice occurs when somebody shouts "thief, thief," in a busy part of a city and a crowd gathers, beats up the victim thoroughly and then proceed to douse him or her with combustible substance like petrol before setting ablaze.

All these are done in a matter of minutes, so the victim may not have the opportunity to make his or her case how much less get legal defense. So it is the first person to raise alarm and shouts the loudest that gets justice from the mob in a jungle situation. Dispensing justice in this way is a very crude and barbaric, it is welcomed by the populace, but source of concern for well-informed men and women.

This brand of justice is hailed by the masses. Here people are like the ancient Greeks, who enjoyed brutish gladiator shows, whereby strong men stabbed each other to death for the amusement of the King and the masses. Rather, they acquiesced with jungle justice due to their ignorance of the fact that the rules and norms that guide modern society today have outlawed some practices that make it difficult to differentiate between mankind and animal from early days to modern days of liberal democracy.

Psychologists would admit that, it is natural for ordinary folks to rejoice over the pain, especially in a country where the leadership has consistently disappointed the followers to the extent that there is no more trust between them.

For both categories of people—the victim and the witnesses—a single incident is a traumatic experience whose effects last throughout their lifetime. This is because the average human mind is not equipped to withstand a high degree of psychological violence. Consequently, in incidents of mob justice, the number of people who are exposed to severe psychological trauma is very high. If not over generalizing or exaggerating, an increase in mob justice in any country means there are more people suffering from psychological trauma in that country. Given the high number of incidents of mob justice in India, hundreds of Indians today suffer from psychological trauma associated with partaking in the incident or by witnessing it.

Lynching was never about justice. It was about terror used to enforce white supremacy

Human beings are basically social and our lives are inter connected and we are childish if we think we can (or do) exist alone. The concept of the 'self' is quite new. Rosa Luxemburg said: "Freedom is always and exclusively freedom for the one who thinks differently." It may mean, not that we should act however we feel regardless of the effect it has on society and the people around us, but that we should respect the rights of others even if we don't want to live in the same way.

Psychological Mindset of a Society

In the days when a portion of the Indian junta is deeply fascinated by the concept of *Gandhigiri*, mob justice looks like a slap on the cheek of those who believe in candle light vigils and silent protests. Unfortunately, turning the other cheek only empowers those sworn to public violence as a means of venting their ire. The vigilantes are only too happy to oblige.

An incident of mob justice, in addition to being a shocking indicator of the psychological mindset of a society, also suggests a failed justice delivery mechanism and the loss of faith of the people in their justice system. If an alarming number of incidents of mob justice are reported from a particular region or country, it strongly suggests that there is something terribly wrong in the societal framework and its justice delivery mechanisms.

It is an inherent part of human nature to instantaneously decide what is good and evil. However, it is not by nature a primordial human trait to decide what punishment is just for a crime and what is not. It is because of this human shortcoming and because of a number of other reasons, like maintaining order, that human society, irrespective of race, ethnicity and region, has evolved various forms of mechanisms for rendering justice throughout history.

When an offense is alleged against a person, irrespective of time and region, there were, and are, mechanisms that decided the punishment, however just or unjust the punishment may be. The societies that practiced mob justice lacked order, and the perception of justice was reduced to a very minimal level of an eye for an eye. It appears that India is unfortunately headed toward turning the whole of India blind.

The lynching of notorious criminal Akku Yadav inside a Nagpur court room in broad day light, three years ago, demonstrated the manner in which several citizens intervened to mete out justice to hapless women. Notably, despite a heavy cordon meant to protect Akku, mob justice ensured that scores of men and women could make their way inside and finish him using unconventional weapons. Akku and his accomplices, in 15 years of their criminal history, reportedly raped over 40 women in the age group of 10 to 40 years.

The above incidents depict public impatience for a plethora of reasons which makes them resort to mob or street or instant justice in the country; many questions have no easy answers. Why that is there are people who are waiting for an opportunity to unleash the criminal element in them and destroy public and private property? What is it that makes ordinary people take the law into their own hands? It is sheer desperation? Or is it that the criminals manage to get away unpunished? Why is the mob ready to pounce on suspected criminals and hoodlums so as to deliver instant street justice?

Some seem to argue that people argue that mob justice discourages people from stealing and so saves the authorities the time and money of prosecution.

Others are quick to point out that mob justice is not the answer to stealing and it not justice at all.

Why do mobs behave in such extreme ways? Various studies have concluded that beyond anger exploding in gruesome violence, it is the manifestation of deep and widespread frustration. It is also attributed to the loosening of normal constraints on behaviour when people are in a crowd, leading to an increase in impulsive and deviant acts. Since groups have been found to encourage a sense of anonymity among its members, this anonymity can often result in 'mob psychology' apart from other anti-social behaviours. Consequently, the presence of a group influence has a large impact on individual behaviours.

Primarily, riots develop a life of their own once they begin. In the first stage of the riot, it is an attack on property. Next people are attacked. When the riot grows and more people join in, the duration of the riot depends on the resistance met by rioters, their organisation and leadership. Due to several factors, the riot may also spread to other areas, sometimes distant from the precipitating site.

Criminals have Human Rights

In his book, The Psychology of Group Aggression, Arnold P. Goldstein, has defined a mob as 'a crowd acting under strong emotional conditions that often lead to violence or illegal acts.' While a riot is 'an instance of mob violence, with the destruction of property or looting, or violence against people, mobs are the product of a process of evolution, formed by people sharing the same 'conscious or unconscious needs.' Riots need a 'trigger' or a 'precipitating event' to begin. Notably, riots have been found to begin well before violence breaks out with broad, non-specific factors, including media sensationalism. If individuals participate in a mob, they do so because of a sense of deprivation.

Even known criminals have human rights. Most importantly, for the law to take its course, political will is imperative.

Once the impact of seeing the photographs of lynched men and women has been absorbed, what begins to dominant is the image of the spectators. This in turn invites viewers to examine our own position as spectators when viewing these images.

"Cognitive dissonance" refers to the discomfort that most people feel when they simultaneously hold two irreconcilable ideas. Dissonance occurs when you recognize at some level that your behaviour contradicts your core beliefs or when you are confronted with factual evidence inconsistent with such beliefs. The resulting discomfort must be resolved. Some people do so by changing their professed beliefs or by revising their original beliefs to fairly account for the new factual evidence. But many, perhaps most, people "*will engage in the most amazing mental gymnastics, all to justify their hypocrisy.* Rephrased, many people will revise their core beliefs to justify (rather than change) their seemingly contradictory behaviour. Likewise, they will find rationalizations to avoid giving up their core beliefs rather than accepting the implications of contrary proof. It is not known why some people react to dissonance with serious introspection while others just rationalize.

Defining lynching—is vigilante justice, and a leading historian defines lynching as "murder endorsed by community.

Lynching Is the Execution of a presumed offender by a mob without trial, under the pretense of administering justice. It sometimes involves torturing the victim and mutilating the body. Lynching has often occurred under unsettled social conditions. The term derives from the name of Charles Lynch, a Virginian who headed an irregular court to persecute loyalists during the American Revolution. In the United States, lynching was widely used in the post-Reconstruction South against blacks, often to intimidate other blacks from exercising their civil rights.

A mob is the most dangerous thing one can get caught in. A mob has no leader, has no logic or reason, and no sense of right or wrong or morals. People who as individuals would not do bad things will certainly do them if they are in a mob where responsibility is diluted and spur of the moment actions happen.

From the above, it is clear that mobs are not limited to hundreds or thousands of people in the street chanting slogans because of a political or religious reason. Some mob behaviour can be exhibited in smaller groups (*e.g.* a group of soldiers in war, who think there is no law, and are encouraged by others behaving badly, and again diluted responsibility).

We also see mob behaviour in situations such as sports fans going on a rampage and destroying property and even killing people.

Negatives of groups:

- Mob behaviour & de-individuation
- Pluralistic ignorance
- Conformity
- Compliance
- Obedience

Mob behaviour we see it after:

- Sports games
- Riots
- Others'

Mob Psychology is a theoretical approach attempting to explain collective behaviour solely on the basis of the psychological states of people who participate. Mob Psychology is similar to terms such as: crowd psychology and group mentality. It is portrayed in many works of literature, including William Shakespeare's *Julius Caesar*.

Mob psychology shows that individuals tend to behave in a different manner as part of a group in contrast to acting independently. Members of a group are prone to acting in ways that they would deem immoral or unjust if in control of their behaviour. This is not due to change in one's belief or principle, but rather the fact that individuals tend to ignore or avoid one's conscience or rational judgement. It can be said that individuals in a group defer their goals and take upon the identity of the group. Therefore, members of a group are likely to commit acts they would never commit alone. Being in a group allows individuals to defer blame, responsibility, accountability, and/or judgement upon the group.

There exist many evidence and examples of mob psychology in modern society. One example is the persecution of the Jews during the Holocaust. The Nazi party blamed Germany's weak economy at the time upon the Jews. Experts and scholars have long pondered how an entire nation came to persecute their Jewish neighbors. Jews were harassed and treated with the utmost insolence. Finally, after several years of worsening persecution, millions were shipped to work camps and either gassed or starved to death. Another example is the Ku Klux Klan (KKK), uniting under the principles of Anglo-Saxon pride, nationalism, and segregration. The Ku-Klux-Klan persecuted African-Americans, promoting segregation under Jim Crow laws, and even murdered innocent people. Both the Nazis and members of the KKK feel that their race is superior to others' and united under a common identity. Nazis had numerous symbols and emblems that they bore, and the KKK dressed in white cloaks and hoods, masking their identity. Books that have been written that exhibit mob psychology include Lord of the Flies by William Golding and George Orwell's 1984.

Mob psychology shows that individuals tend to behave in a different manner as part of a group in contrast to acting independently. Members of a group are prone to acting in ways that they would deem immoral or unjust if in control of their behaviour. This is not due to change in one's belief or principle, but rather the fact that individuals tend to ignore or avoid one's conscience or rational judgment. It can be said that individuals in a group defer their goals and take upon the identity of the group. Therefore, members of a group are likely to commit acts they would never commit alone. Being in a group allows individuals to defer blame, responsibility, accountability, and/or judgment upon the group

The *noun* lynching has one meaning: putting to death by mob action without due process of law

A World Picture

Between the end of Reconstruction (mid-1870s) and World War II, there were some 3,500 documented incidents of lynching and mob violence against African Americans, most of them in the South. The victims, mostly men, were not only hung, but often also tortured, their bodies displayed publicly and/or dismembered for grisly souvenirs. Sometimes these men had been convicted of a crime, sometimes only accused, and sometimes even acquitted, but the real point was to terrorize the communities in which African Americans lived. Although the participants in the mob rarely hid their identities, few were ever arrested, let alone punished for their crimes; in fact, according to police reports, grand jury investigations, and newspaper accounts, the African American victims met their fates "at the hands of parties unknown."

Documented the Events

Photographs of lynching "parties" reveal that members of the mob or audience often posed with the corpses of their victims, in a sort of trophy shot akin to those of successful hunters and fishermen. In some cases, these macabre photographs were hawked from home to home and town to town, a way for the photographers to make money and for whites who could not be present to participate vicariously in the expression of power the pictures represented. On occasion, the photos were turned into postcards which could be mailed to friends and relatives in distant locations. In these ways, these lynching photographs themselves served as an important element in the maintenance of a racial hierarchy that asserted that all whites deserved to stand above all blacks. After viewing one such photograph in 1935, composer and civil rights activist James Weldon Johnson remarked that lynching was a "problem of saving black America's body and white America's soul."

In the 1980s, James Allen, a white southerner sympathetic to the struggle against racism, began to collect these photographs and postcards while making his rounds of antique and junk shops, flea markets, and private dealers across the South. The images captured the horrible history of lynching in trees, bridges, and towers, and atop bonfires. He also purchased posed shots of the mobs, their members staring unabashedly into the camera's lens. As Allen's collection grew, the idea of exhibiting the images publicly occurred to him, and, in 1999, they made their first appearance in a small museum in New York City—thirty-odd worn snapshots and postcards, collectively titled "Without Sanctuary."

Eventually transferred to the New York Historical Society, where a collection of anti-lynching movement tracts, posters, and materials from the 1890s through the 1930s were added, with notebooks provided for viewers to record their thoughts and emotions.

The photographs have been every bit as controversial as the exhibit has been popular. Some critics warned of the risk of victimizing the victims once again, this time by showing their painful images, and of the danger of creating a new pornography of violence and torture. Other critics suggested that the photographs encouraged viewers to adopt the gaze of mob participants, to identify with the evil-doers. There was also the possibility that white supremacist groups would themselves celebrate the lynchings and appropriate the images to post on their websites (they have done so). And then there were people who argued that the images were just too horrific to be viewed or that their display might generate racial hostilities where "progress" had been made. On the other hand, there were also scholars, activists, and curators who were interested in displaying the exhibit, and they called for it to tour museums and universities.

In early October 2002, Emory University hosted a conference entitled "Lynching and Racial Violence: Histories and Legacies," which attracted more than 200 scholars from undergraduate and graduate students, to young professors and senior scholars from every imaginable academic field—history, sociology, political science, law, English, art, theater, music, religious studies, and philosophy—and 121 institutions—community colleges, private liberal arts colleges, and public research universities. There were also many community activists, from communities around the country, who have made their top priority the memorialization of places of racial violence. The lynch mobs could never have anticipated that someday such brainpower and passion would be loosed in response to the pain they had inflicted.

Controversy about the Term Lynching

There were sharp differences of opinion about what is meant by the term "lynching." Some argued that a lynching must involve a mob taking the law into their own hands, killing one or more victims, and often following a ritualized procedure. Proponents of this definition also contend that most lynchings occurred between the 1870s and the 1930s. They preferred to use the categories "racial violence" and "domestic terrorism," and they argued that such practices began during slavery (the uses of violence, whipping, maiming, torture, rape, punitive sales, and the like), took on the forms of community-based violence called "lynchings" in the years of Jim Crow (1870s through the 1940s), and then were assumed by the government itself as police brutality and capital punishment. These critics question the formal distinctions between legal and extra-legal violence, pointing to the presence of police officials in the lynching photos, taking note of the failure of local authorities to prosecute participants in lynchings and the unwillingness, time and again, of all three branches of the federal government (executive, legislative, and judicial) to intervene to outlaw lynching, and citing statistics that reveal the disproportionate punishment of all people of color.

Not one scholarly book on lynching had been published between 1945 and 1975. But recent years have seen dissertations, books, and articles which probed lynchings, racial pogroms (attacks on black communities), and state-sanctioned violence, making possible a new narrative of the course of U.S. history. Oral folklore kept the reports of murder and torture alive within African American families and communities.

Chapter 2

The Fabric of Indian Society

The Indian social structure and cultural pattern are characterized by unity as well as diversity. Historically, India has been hospitable to numerous groups of immigrants from different parts of Asia and Europe, but the culture of each group has undergone enough change over the centuries to become an integral part of the Indian mosaic. The institution of caste may be mentioned as a typical example of the paradox that is Indian society. Each caste stands for a way of life that is to some extent distinctive, but at the same time the castes of a region form part of a single social framework. It is important to note that caste is found not only among the Hindus but also among the Muslims, Christians, Sikhs, Jains and Jews. Caste is ubiquitous, and this has resulted in an ideology tolerant of diversity.

Factors making for diversity are apparent even to the casual observer. The population of India is racially diverse, containing elements from six main racial types: the Negrito, the Proto-Australoid, the Mongoloid, the Mediterranean, the Western Brachycephals, and the Nordic. All the great religions of the world are represented in this country. The tribal groups enjoy varying degrees of contact with one or the other of the great religions. The major literary languages alone number fourteen. Diversity is seen in the patterns of rural as well as urban settlements, community life, forms of land tenure and agricultural operations. In kinship, marriage rites and customs, inheritance, and the general mode of living, there are striking differences between groups.

Diversity is, however, only one side of the picture. There are unifying factors as well. India is a political entity, every part of which is under the same Constitution. The process of unification developed as several great rulers Asoka, Samudragupta, Akbar—brought large parts of the country under their power; but it was only during British rule that India became for the first time a single political entity.

The concept of the unity of India is inherent in Hinduism. There are sacred centres of Hindu pilgrimage in every corner of the land. Certain salient aspects of Sanskritic culture are to be found all over the country. India is the sacred land not only of the Hindus but also of the Sikhs, Jains and Buddhists. The Muslims and Christians, too, have several sacred centres of pilgrimage in India. The institution of caste cuts across diverse religious groups and gives them all a common social idiom.

The declaration of India as a secular State provides one more evidence of the tolerance of diversity which has been characteristic of Indian history from its beginning. The process of economic development ushered in by the Five Year Plans and the spread of egalitarian ideals have brought about revolutionary changes in the Indian pattern of social life. A single government and a common body of civil and criminal law, a developing economy, and a secular approach to public life and problems are now providing substance and reality to India's claim to be a nation.

STRUCTURE OF INDIAN SOCIETY

The Caste System

The first literary traces of the caste system are to be found in the Rig-Veda, where three groups are mentioned: Brdkma (Priests), Ksatra (Kings or Rulers), and Vis (common people). The Purusasukta hymn, however, speaks of four classes originating from four parts of the body of the Creator. These classes, Brahmana, Rajanya, Vaisya and Sudra, are referred to in later literature as Caturvarna. The term varna does not seem to have been applied to these classes in the earliest literature, except to contrast the fair Arya with the dark Dasa. The initial distinction of people into two varnas later developed into three {Brahma, Ksatra and Vis) and finally into four. The occupations of the first two varnas are clearly stated to be priesthood, and administrative and military duties, respectively. But the duties of the Vaisya and Sudra are not very clear. The village headman was usually a Vaisya, and Sudras were servants. The Varna categories do not, however, exhaust the various occupations practised in Vedic India. The Rig-Veda, for instance, mentions several occupations by name—chariot-builder, goldsmith, barber, physician, leather-worker, potter, merchant and others. The question arises whether these occupations referred to endogamous jatis as we know them today. It is not known how they fitted into the varna framework.

The *post-Vedic period saw the growth and consolidation of the power of the Brahmins*. Brahmin writers continually discussed and denned the duties and rights of each caste and its place in the hierarchy. (The relation which these writings bore to the empirical reality is not clear). *Justifications and rationalizations* of the hierarchy were also produced during this period. In the *Bhagavad-Gita,* for instance, the caste system is sought to be justified on the basis of the ideas of *guna, karma* and *dharma.*

The 6th, century B.C. saw the rise of Buddhism, which is believed to have questioned the basis of the caste system itself. Some scholars, however, have said that Buddhism on its social and political side was chiefly a Ksatriya movement against Brahminical supremacy.

Post-Vedic Brahminical writers continued their attempts to systematize and codify inter-caste relations. The idea of pollution was elaborated to define the distance separating the castes. Violations of caste rules were punished either by the village panchayat or the panchayat of the locally dominant caste or by the king.

The Bhakti movement with its long history contained elements which ran counter to caste ideology. The Bhakti saints came from all castes, including the Harijans. It appears as though the path of *Bhakti* offered a way out of the tyrannies of the caste system, and as the Bhakti saints commanded respect from every one, the movement itself served to stress the worth of an individual irrespective of his caste affiliations. The origins of the Bhakti movement are traced to the Kisna-Vasudeva cult in the first century B.C. The Saiva (Nayanar) and Vaisnava (Alvar) saints of the Tamil country, the Haridasas and Lingayat saints of Karnataka. Vallabhacarya and his followers in Gujarat, Caitanya in Bengal, and Tulasi das, Surd as, Kabir and Ramanand in the North, were all representatives of the Bhakti movement. The movement was more or less continuous in Indian history, and it spread right across the subcontinent. It may not be too fanciful to regard it as a protest, in the realm of religion, against the division of human beings into high and low castes.

The *Lingayat movement*, which came into existence in Karnataka in the 12th century A.D., rejected many ideas of traditional Hinduism, including *karma,* ritualism and caste. It also emphasized the necessity as well as the dignity of labour. The movement attracted converts from all castes including Harijans. But over the centuries it became a congeries of small, endogamous *jails.* The followers of Kabir (Kablrpanthi) also became a caste. Caste even survived conversion to Christianity and Islam. During the last century there came into existence the Arya Samaj) in the Punjab and the Brahma Samaj in Bengal. These movements, as well as the Ramakrishna Mission, represented a shift towards the liberalization of caste.

Main Features

We shall now consider the main features of caste before it was deeply affected by recent changes. Those changes, which present a quite different picture of the Indian social structure today, are discussed in the last pages of this chapter.

The features of caste prevailing: through the past centuries may be described under nine heads: hierarchy; endogamy and hypergamy; occupational association; restriction on food, drink and smoking; distinction in custom, dress and speech; pollution; ritual and other privileges and disabilities; caste organization and caste mobility.

The essence of caste is the arrangement of hereditary groups in a hierarchy. The popular impression of the hierarchy is a clear-cut one, derived from the idea of *varna,* with Brahmins at the top and Harijans at the bottom. But, as a matter of fact, only the two opposite ends of the hierarchy are relatively fixed; in between, and especially in the middle regions, there is considerable room for debate regarding mutual position. In a dispute over rank each caste would cite as evidence of its superiority the items of its dietary, the other caste groups from which it accepted or refused to accept cooked food and water, the ritual it performed and the customs it observed, its traditional privileges and disabilities, and the myth of its origin. The fact that mutual position is arguable, if not vague, over great areas of the hierarchy permits social mobility. Mobility, it may be noted, is not a recent phenomenon. Even in the traditional system it was possible for a caste to move up. The Raj Gonds of Central India, for instance, successfully claimed for themselves the rank of Ksatriyas on the basis of their acquisition of political power. At the coronation of Sivajl, Brahmin priests declared him a Ksatriya. Not infrequently the claim of a caste to a higher rank is not conceded. Thus, v/the Smith group of castes in South India have claimed to be a twice-born caste and call themselves Visvakarma Brahmin. The other castes resent this and even the Harijans do not accept drinking water from a Smith. The Linguists consider themselves superior to the Brahmins but others do not accept their claim.

Disputes regarding mutual position occur even at either extremes of the hierarchy. In Kerala, Nambutris consider themselves superior to Tamil Brahmins, and among the Nambutris those who have a hereditary right to study the Vedas claim superiority over the others. Again, there are very low groups among the Brahmins. No caste, including the Harijan, will accept cooked food or water from the Marka Brahmins of Mysore. Likewise, the Vatima Brahmins in the Tamil country and the Tapodhan Brahmins in Gujarat are considered as inferior.

All Caste Hindus regard Harijans as being at the bottom rung of the ladder. But the category of Harijans is not homogeneous. In each linguistic area there are a. few Harijan castes which form a hierarchy. The leather-working Camar in Uttar Pradesh considers himself superior to the Bhangi, a sweeper. The Kannada Holey a places himself above the Madiga; he proudly stresses the fact that he does not accept even water or betel leaf from either the Smith or the Marka Brahmin.

Conflict ought to be seen as inhering in social life everywhere. The institutional devices which every society has provided for the solution of conflict may work with greater or less efficiency. Or the devices may work efficiently in some areas and not in others. There may be more conflict in some societies than in others, and in the same society there may be more conflict in some periods in the same society there may be more conflict in some periods than in the others. Conflict may be uniform over almost the entire range of institutions, or more frequent in some than in the others. It may be much greater over some objects and events than over others. But conflict as such is an inescapable part of social existence, and should be of serious concern to the sociologist.

It is necessary to distinguish between form of conflict that can be resolved by existing institutional mechanisms, and more fundamental conflicts that threaten that entire social order. The social order may change gradually over a period of time, or suddenly and with violence. The suddenness of the change may however, be more apparent than real, the dynamic forces having gone unrecognized for some time or their significance having been misunderstood.

The developing countries are characterized by the existence of leaders who are determined to bring about radical changes in traditional life and culture, and these leaders both reflect and guide the aspirations, hopes, and ideals of their followers, Populations.

The sociologist's commitment to democratic processes is fundamental, and is derived from his commitment to his discipline, for unfettered social inquiry cannot exist and flourish in totalitarian systems. This is particularly true in regard to a sociologist studying his own society. Commitment to democratic processes results in the sociologist having a deep concern in national development; the expectations of ordinary people have risen everywhere, and they can only be satisfied by swift development as well as by a swift and sharp reduction of existing inequalities. Development which only makes the rich richer and leaves the condition of the masses of the poor unchanged is likely to produce chronic political instability which, in turn, will hamstring development. Commitment to development is therefore also a commitment to the reduction of economic and social inequalities.

What is a Caste System?

A caste system is a social system where people are ranked into groups based on heredity within rigid systems of social stratification, especially those that constitute Hindu India. Some scholars, in fact, deny that true caste systems are found outside India. The caste is a closed group whose members are severely restricted in their choice of occupation and degree of social participation. Marriage outside the caste is prohibited. Social status is determined by the caste of one's birth and may only rarely be transcended. Certain religious minorities may voluntarily constitute a quasi-caste within a society, but they are less apt to be characterized by cultural distinctiveness than by their self-imposed social segregation. A specialized labour group may operate as a caste within a society otherwise free of such distinctions (*e.g.*, the ironsmiths in parts of Africa). In general, caste functions to maintain the status quo in a society.

Castes in India

Designates a group varying in size from a handful to many thousands. There are thousands of such jatis, and each has its distinctive rules, customs, and modes of government. The term varna (literally meaning "color") refers to the ancient and somewhat ideal fourfold division of Hindu society:

1. the Brahmans, the priestly and learned class;
2. the Kshatriyas, the warriors and rulers;
3. the Vaisyas, farmers and merchants; and
4. the Sudras, peasants and labourers. These divisions may have corresponded to what were formerly large, broad, undifferentiated social classes.

Below the category of Sudras were the untouchables, or Panchamas (literally "fifth division"), who performed the most menial tasks.

Although there has been much confusion between the two, jati and varna are different in origin as well as function. The various castes in any given region of India are hierarchically organized, with each caste corresponding roughly to one or the other of the varna categories. Traditionally, caste mobility has taken the form of movement up or down the varna scale. Indian castes are rigidly differentiated by rituals and beliefs that pervade all thought and conduct. Extreme upper and lower castes differ so widely in habits of everyday life and worship that only the close intergrading of intervening castes and the intercaste language communities serve to hold them together within the single framework of Indian society.

The explanation that Indian castes were originally based on color lines to preserve the racial and cultural purity of conquering groups is inadequate historically to account for the physical and cultural variety of such groups. Castes may reflect distinctiveness of religious practice, occupation, locale, culture status, or tribal affiliation, either exclusively or in part. Divergence within a caste on any of these lines will tend to produce fission that may, in time, result in the formation of new castes. Every type of social group as it appears may be fitted into this system of organizing society.

The occupational barriers among Indian castes have been breaking down slowly under economic pressures since the 19th cent., but social distinctions have been more persistent. Attitudes toward the untouchables only began to change in the 1930s under the influence of Mohandas Gandhi's teachings. Although un-touch ability was declared illegal in 1949, resistance to change has remained strong, especially in rural areas. As increased industrialization produced new occupations and new social and political functions evolved, the caste system adapted and thus far has not been destroyed.

"An Eye for an Eye"

The guiding philosophy in today's India increasingly not the penal code but the Old Testament's Mosaic Law—"*An Eye for an Eye" and "A Tooth for a Tooth*".

Accept it or not, India has two kinds of criminal judicial systems at play in the country and at the moment they do not connect. The first and most over arching one of course is the British imposed penal code. This supposedly is the only officially sanctioned system and has a hierarchy built up right from the session's courts to the High Courts and then the Supreme Court; Then are the traditional Panchayats—typically the caste panchayats .

Now a caste Panchayat might look abhorrent to the reformed modern mind, but caught between a anesthetized "modern judiciary" which has heaps of paper work and years of hearing before it can hand down a sentence which can then be appealed and vigilante justice which kills and shoots the first person in sight and only contributes to anarchy, caste panchayats operate within known and generally understood social norms, convene with minimal fuss and its verdicts are instantly enforced.

The traditional panchayat has teeth and authority. Admittedly, this is an institution more often than not guided by medieval norms which are reactionary and retrogressive but remember the so called "modern judicial system" that we so proudly flaunt actually dates back to the nineteenth century and whereas the penal code is cast in concrete so to speak, the social mores and norms evolve, albeit they evolve slowly.

If we have to escape vigilante folk justice which is totally mindless, we have to reform our judicial system. By paying attention to the modern judicial system alone, we have set up special courts, evening courts, Fast Track Courts, mobile courts, CBI courts and all sorts of other courts but none of this works for they are the legal system of the elite and the poor small fish who get caught in its net unless they can afford expensive lawyers are doomed. On the other hand, the traditional panchayats which require no lawyers, no costly court rooms, no paraphernalia have received little attention and attempts at modernization. Doesn't the traditional judicial system deserve a chance with some inputs in terms of trying to bring it up to speed from its current medieval moorings? Sensational journalism spares the public no detail no matter how horrible. In mob justice people accused of a crime are left at the hands of angry and irrational people who were less interested in justice

Chapter 3

Collective Behaviour

Studying collective behaviour is difficult for several reasons, including:

1. Collective behaviour is wide-ranging.
2. Collective behaviour is complex.
3. Much collective behaviour is transitory.

A *collectivity* is *a large number of people whose minimal interaction occurs in the absence of well-defined conventional norms.* Two different types of collectivities are identified: *dispersed collectivity* or *mass behaviour,* and *localized collectivity.* Collectivities are distinguished from social groups on the basis of three characteristics:

- Collectivities are based on limited social interaction.
- Collectivities have no clear social boundaries.
- Collectivities generate weak and unconventional norms.

Localized Collectivities: Crowds

A *crowd* is *a temporary gathering of people who share a common focus of attention and who influence one another.* Herbert Blumer identified four types of crowds, based in part on their level of emotional intensity. These include: the *casual crowd,* the *conventional crowd,* the *expressive crowd,* and the *acting crowd.* The author adds a fifth type of crowd—the *protest crowd.* This latter type of crowd is distinguished from the other four by the variability of emotions between its participants.

Mobs and Riots: When an acting crowd becomes violent it is classified as a *mob,* or *a highly emotional crowd that pursues a violent or destructive goal.* Lynching is a notorious example in the history of the Nations.

Mob

A mob is usually a group of people that has taken the law into their own hands. Mobs are usually a group which gather temporarily for a particular reason.

A frenzied crowd without any particular purpose is a *riot,* or *a social eruption that is highly emotional, violent, and undirected.* Throughout history riots have resulted from a collective expression against social injustice. Riots are not always fired by hate.

Crowds, Mobs, and Social Change: Over history, crowds have been able to affect social change, and have also provoked controversy. Ordinary people can gain power through collective activity.

Explaining Crowd Behaviour

Contagion Theory: *Contagion theory* maintains that crowds can exert a hypnotic effect over their members. The anonymity within a crowd encourages people to abandon personal responsibility, which stirs up emotions and drives people toward irrational, even violent, action.

Convergence Theory The idea behind *convergence theory* is that people of like mind come together for a particular purpose and form a crowd. Crowd behaviour is not irrational; rather, people in crowds express existing beliefs and values.

Emergent-Norm Theory: Ralph Turner and Lewis Killian developed the *emergent-norm theory,* of crowd dynamics. This view represents the use of symbolic-interaction paradigm. Crowd behaviour is neither as irrational as contagion theory suggests, nor as deliberate as convergence theory implies. Crowd behaviour reflects the desires of participants but is also guided by norms that emerge as the situation unfolds.

Dispersed Collectivities: Mass Behaviour

Mass behaviour refers to collective behaviour among people dispersed over a wide geographic area.

Rumor and *Gossip Rumor* is unsubstantiated information people spread informally, often by word of mouth. Rumor has three essential characteristics:

- It thrives in a climate of ambiguity,
- It is unstable, and
- It is difficult to stop.

Closely related to rumor is *gossip*, or *rumor about people's personal affairs*. It can be an effective means of social control.

Public Opinion and Propaganda: *Public opinion* is a form of highly dispersed collective behaviour. No one "public opinion" exists on key social issues, but rather is represented by a diversity of opinion. However, sharing particular traits in common with others can create certain patterns in attitudes.

A public grows larger and smaller over time as interest in a particular issue changes. Certain categories of people have more social influence than others when it comes to shaping public opinion.

Propaganda is defined as *information presented with the intention of shaping public opinion.* While *information* is used to enlighten, *propaganda* is used to sway an audience toward some viewpoint. A fine line exists between the two.

Panic and Mass Hysteria: A *panic* is *a form of localized collective behaviour by which people react to a threat or other stimulus with irrational, frantic, and often self-destructive behaviour;* People streaming toward the exits in a crowded theater after someone yells "fire" is a classic example.

Mass hysteria is *a form of dispersed collective behaviour by which people react to a real or imagined event with irrational, frantic, and often self-destructive behaviour.*

Fashions and Fads *Fashion* is *a social pattern favored by a large number of people.* Fashions reflect basic cultural values and tend to evolve over time.

U.S. sociologist Thorstein Veblen originated the term *conspicuous consumption,* referring to the practice of spending money with the intention of displaying one's wealth to others.

A *fad* is *an unconventional social pattern that people embrace briefly but enthusiastically.* They are sometimes referred to as *crazes.* While fads are truly "passing fancies," fashions become incorporated into a society's culture.

Social Movements

Three characteristics differentiate social movements from other types of collective behaviour: a higher degree of internal organization; typically longer duration, often spanning many years; and the deliberate attempt to reorganize society itself.

While rare in pre-industrial societies, social movements are common in industrialized societies. They develop around a wide range of social issues.

Social Relationship

The term "social relationship" will be used for the meaning-content by which a circle of persons *relates* each other and to which their behaviours are oriented. The social relationship thus *consists* entirely and exclusively in the existence of a probability that there will be, in some meaningfully understandable sense, a course of social action.

The meaning of a social relationship may be *agreed* upon by mutual consent. This implies that the parties make *promises* covering their future behaviour, whether toward each other or toward third persons. In such cases each party then normally counts, if he or she acts rationally, in some degree on the fact that the *other*'s action will orient to the meaning of the agreement as he or she (the first actor) understands it. In part, they orient their action end-rationally to these expectations, to be sure, varying degrees of subjectively "faithful" intention of doing their part. But in part also they are motivated each by the value-rationality of the "duty" to adhere to the agreement in the sense in which he or she understands it. This much may be *anticipated.*

CONFLICT RELATIONSHIP

Types of Conflict

A social relationship will be called "*conflict*" if social action is oriented intentionally to carrying out the actor's own will against the resistance of the other party or parties. The term "peaceful" conflict is applied to cases in which actual physical force is not employed. A peaceful conflict is "competition" if it consists in a formally peaceful attempt to attain controlling power over opportunities which are also desired by others. A competition will be called "regulated" if its ends and means are oriented to an order. The struggle, often latent, which takes place between human individuals or types of life opportunity, for advantages and for survival, but without a meaningful mutual orientation in terms of conflict, will be called "selection." If it is a matter of the living opportunities of individuals during their own lifetime, it will be called "social selection"; if it concerns differential chances for the survival of inherited characteristics, it will be called "biological selection."

Conflict and Order

There are all manner of continuous transitions ranging from the bloody type of conflict which, setting aside all rules, aims at the destruction of the adversary, to the case of the battles of medieval chivalry, bound as they were to the strictest conventions, and to the strict regulations imposed on sport by the rules of the game. A classic example of conventional regulation even in war is the herald's call before the battle of Fontenoy (1745): "English gentlemen, shoot first." There are transitions such as that from unregulated competition of, let us say, suitors for the favor of a woman to the competition for economic advantages in exchange relationships, bound as that is by the order governing the market, or to strictly regulated competitions for artistic awards or, finally, to the struggle for victory in election campaigns. The treatment of conflict involving the use of physical violence as a separate type is justified by the special characteristics of the employment of this means and the corresponding peculiarities of the sociological consequences of its use.

All typical struggles and common competition which take place on a large scale will lead, in the long run, despite the decisive importance in many individual cases of accidental factors and luck, to a selection of those who have in the higher degree, on the average, possessed the personal qualities important to success. What qualities are important depends on the conditions in which the conflict or competition takes place. It may be a matter of physical strength or of unscrupulous cunning, of the level of mental concentration or mere lung power and skill in the technique of demagoguery, of loyalty to superiors or to the masses, of creative originality, or of adaptability, of qualities which are unusual, or of those which are possessed by the mediocre majority. Among the decisive conditions, it must not be forgotten, belong the types of *order* to which the behaviour of the parties is oriented, whether traditional, value-rational or end-rational. *Each* type of order influences opportunities in the process of social selection differently.

Selection and Conflict

Not *every* process of social selection is, in the present sense, a case of conflict. Social selection, on the contrary, means only in the first instance that certain types of behaviour, and hence of the corresponding personal qualities, are more favorable than others in procuring differential advantages in attaining to certain social *relationships*, as in the role of "lover," "husband," "member of parliament," "official," "contractor," "managing director," "successful business person," and so on. But the concept does not specify whether this differential advantage in selection for social success is brought to bear through conflict or not, neither does it specify whether the biological chances of survival of the type are affected one way or the other. It is only where there is a genuine *competitive process* that the term conflict will be used.

It is only in the sense of "selection" that it seems, according to our experience, that conflict is empirically *inevitable*, and it is furthermore only in the sense of *biological* selection that it is inevitable in *principle*. Selection is inevitable because apparently no way can be worked out of eliminating it completely. It is possible even for the most strictly pacific order to eliminate means of conflict and the objects of and impulses to conflict only in that it deals with each type individually. But this means that *other* modes of conflict would come to the fore, possibly in processes of open competition. But even on the utopian assumption that all competition were completely eliminated, conditions would still lead to a latent process of selection, biological or social, which would favor the types best adapted to the conditions, whether their relevant qualities were mainly conditioned by heredity or by environment. On an empirical level the elimination of conflict cannot go beyond a point which leaves room for some social selection, and in principle a process of biological selection necessarily remains.

From the struggle of *individuals* for personal advantages and survival, it is naturally necessary to distinguish the "conflict" and the "selection" of social *relationships*. It is only in a metaphorical sense that these concepts can be applied to the latter. For "relationships" *exist* only as particular meaning-content to which human action is oriented. Thus a process of "selection" or a "conflict" between them means only that one type of action has in the course of time been *displaced* by another, whether it is action by the same persons or by others. This may occur in various *ways*.

Selection and Social Relationship

Human action may in the first place be *consciously* aimed to alter certain social relationships—that is, to *alter* the meaning-content of corresponding *action*—or it may be directed to the prevention of their development or continuance. Thus a "state" may be destroyed by war or revolution, or a conspiracy may be broken up by violent suppression; prostitution may be suppressed by police action; "shady" business practices, by denial of legal protection or by penalties. Furthermore, social relationships may be influenced by the conscious creation of differential advantages which favor one type over another. It is possible either for individuals or for many to pursue such ends. Secondly, it may, in various ways, be an unanticipated consequence of a course of social action and its relevant conditions that certain types of social relationships (meaning of the corresponding *actions*) will be adversely affected in their opportunities to maintain themselves or to arise. All changes of natural and social conditions have some sort of effect on the differential probabilities of survival of social relationships. Anyone is at liberty to speak in such cases of a process of "selection" of social relationships. For instance, one may say that among several states the "strongest," in the sense of the best "adapted," is victorious. It must, however, be kept in mind that this so-called "selection" has nothing to do with the selection of *types* of human individuals in either the social or the biological sense. In every case it is necessary to inquire into the *reasons* which have led to a change in the chances of survival of one or another form of social action or social relationship, which has broken up a social relationship or which has permitted it to continue at the expense of other competing forms. The explanation of these processes involves so many factors that it does not seem expedient to employ a single term for them. When this is done, there is always a danger of introducing uncritical *value-judgments* into empirical investigation. There is, above all, a danger of being primarily concerned with justifying the success of an individual case. Since individual cases are often dependent on highly exceptional circumstances, they may be in a certain sense "accidental results." In recent years there has been more than enough of this kind of argument. The fact that a given specific social relationship has been eliminated for reasons peculiar to a particular situation, proves nothing whatever about its "adoptability" in *general* terms.

RATIONAL RELATIONSHIP

A social relationship will be called "rational" if the orientation of social action rests on value—or end-rational *comparison* of *obligation* and interests. It is especially common, though by no means inevitable, for the rational relationship to rest on a mutual *agreement.* In that case the corresponding action is, at the pole of rationality, oriented either to a value-rational belief in *specific* obligation, or to an end-rational expectation of the loyalty of the partner.

The purest cases of rational relationships are: (A) purely end-rational free market exchange, which constitutes a compromise of complementary interests each other; (B) the pure end-rational association, a case of agreement as to a continuing course of action oriented purely to the promotion of specific outer interests, economic or other, of its members; (C) the value-rational association motivated by *inner* interests, for example, the rational sect, if it does not cultivate emotional and affective interests, but seeks only to serve a "cause." This last case, to be sure, seldom occurs in anything approaching the pure type.

COMMUNAL RELATIONSHIP

Definition

A social relationship, on the other hand, will be called "communal" if the orientation of social action—whether in the individual case, on the average, or in the pure type—is based on subjective sentiment of the parties, whether affectual or traditional, that they *belong together*.

Communal relationships may rest on various types of affectual, emotional, or traditional bases. Examples are a religious brotherhood, an erotic relationship, a relation of personal loyalty, a national community, a military corps. The type case is most conveniently illustrated by the family. But the great majority of social relationships has this characteristic to *some degree*, while it is at the same time to *some degree* conditioned by rational factors. No matter how calculating and hard-headed the ruling considerations in such a social relationship—as that of a merchant to one's customers—may be, it is quite possible for it to involve emotional values which transform its utilitarian end. Every social relationship which goes beyond the pursuit of immediate common ends, which hence lasts for long periods, involves relatively enduring social relationships between the same persons, and these cannot be exclusively confined to the technically necessary activities. Hence in such cases as association in the same military unit, in the same school class, in the same workshop or office, there is always some tendency in the communal direction, although the degree, to be sure, varies enormously. Conversely, a social relationship which is normally considered primarily communal may involve action on the part of some or even all of the participants, which is to an important degree oriented to end-rational considerations. There is, for instance, a wide variation in the extent to which the members of a family feel a "community" or, on the other hand, utilize it as "rational relationship" for their own end. The concept of communal relationship has been intentionally defined in very general terms and hence includes very heterogeneous components.

Communion and Conflict

The communal relationship is, according to the usual interpretation of its meaning-content, the most radical antithesis of *conflict*. This should not, however, be allowed to obscure the fact that coercion of all sorts is very common in even the most intimate communal relationships if one party is weaker in character than the other. Furthermore, a process of the "selection" of types leading to differences in opportunity and survival, goes on within these relationships just the same as anywhere else. Rational relationships, on the other hand, very often consist *only* in compromises between conflicting interests, where only *a part of* the occasion or means of conflict has been eliminated, or even an attempt has been made to do so. Hence, outside the area of compromise, the conflict of interests, with its attendant *competition* for supremacy, remains unchanged. Conflict and communal relationships are relative concepts. Conflict varies enormously according to the means employed, especially whether they are violent or peaceful, and to the ruthlessness with which they are used. It has already been pointed out that any type of order governing social action in some way leaves room for a process of 'selection' among various rival human types.

Community, Race and Language

It is by no means true that the existence of *common* qualities, *common* situations, or *common* modes of behaviour imply the existence of a communal relationship. Thus, for instance, a common biological inheritance by which persons are classified as belonging to the same "race," naturally implies no sort of communal relationship between them. By restrictions on social intercourse and on marriage persons may find themselves in a similar situation of isolation from the environment which imposes these distinctions. But even if they all react to this situation in the same way, this does not constitute a communal relationship. The latter does not exist even if they have a common "sentiment" about this situation and its consequences. It is only when this sentiment leads to a mutual *orientation* of their behaviour to each other that a social relationship arises between them, a social relationship to each other and not only to persons in the environment. Furthermore, this relationship is called a "community" only if it involves sentiments of belonging together. In the case of the Jews, for instance, except for Zionist circles and the action of certain associations promoting specifically Jewish interests, there thus exist communal relationships only to a relatively small extent; indeed, Jews often repudiate the existence of a Jewish "community."

Common language, which arises from a similarity of tradition through the family and the surrounding social environment, facilitates mutual understanding, and thus the formation of all types of social relationships, in the highest degree. But it is not sufficient to constitute a communal relationship by itself, but only for the facilitation of intercourse within the groups concerned, thus for the development of rational relationships. In the first place, this takes place between *individuals, not* because they speak the same language, but because they have interests each other. Orientation to the rules of a common language is thus primarily important only as a means of communication, not as the meaning-content of a social relationship. It is only with the emergence of a consciousness of difference from third persons who speak a different language that the fact that two persons speak the same language, and in that respect share a common situation, can lead them to a sentiment of community and to social relationship consciously based on the common language.

MARKET RELATIONSHIP

Participation in a "market" is of still another kind of social relationship. It encourages association between the individual parties to specific acts of exchange and a social relationship, above all that of competition, between the individual participants who must mutually orient their action to each other. But no further social relationship develop except in cases where certain participants enter into agreements in order to better their competitive situations, or where they all agree on rules for the purpose of regulating transactions and of securing favorable general conditions for all. It may further be remarked that the market and the competitive economy resting on it form the most important type of the reciprocal determination of action in terms of direct *interest-situation*, a type which is characteristic of modern economic life.

OPEN AND CLOSED RELATIONSHIP

Definition

A social relationship, regardless of whether it is communal or rational in character, will be spoken of as "*open*" to outsiders if participation in the mutually oriented social action relevant to its meaning-content is, according to its validity of order, not denied to anyone who wishes to participate and who is actually in a position to do so. A relationship will, on the other hand, be called "*closed*" against outsiders if, according to its meaning-content and the validity of its order, participation of certain persons is excluded, limited, or subjected to conditions. Whether a relationship is open or closed may be conditioned traditionally, affectually, value-rationally or end-rationally. (A) Examples of communal relationships, which tend to be closed on a traditional basis, are those membership in which is conditioned by family relationship. (B) Sentimental relationships are usually affectually closed. Examples are erotic relationships and, very commonly, relations of personal loyalty. (C) Relative closure on the basis of value-rationality is usual in strict belief-society. (D) Typical closure on grounds of end-rationality are economic band in a monopolistic or a plutocratic character.

It is especially likely to be closed, for rational reasons, in the following type of situation: a social relationship may provide the parties for opportunities of the satisfaction of various interests, whether the satisfactions be spiritual or material, whether the interest be in the goal of the relationship as such or in some outcome of participation, or whether it is achieved through communal action or by a comparison of interests. If the participants expect that the admission of others will lead to an improvement of their situation, an improvement in degree, in kind, in the security or the value of the satisfaction, their interest will be in keeping the relationship open. If, on the other hand, their expectations are of monopolizing their opportunity, their interest is in a closed relationship.

Examples

A few examples may be taken at random. Whether a group of people engaged in conversation is open or closed depends on its content. General conversation is apt to be open, as contrasted with intimate conversation or business communication. Market relationships are in most, or at least in many, cases essentially open. In the case of many relationships, both communal and rational, there is a tendency to *shift* from a phase of open to one of closure. Examples are the guilds and the democratic city-states of Antiquity and the Middle Ages. At times these groups sought to increase their membership in the interest of improving the security of their position of power by adequate numbers. At other times they restricted their membership to protect the value of their monopolistic position. The same phenomenon is common in monasteries and religious sects which have passed from a stage of religious proselytizing to one of restriction in the interest of the maintenance of an ethical standard or for the protection of material interests. There is a similar relationship between the extensions of market relationships in the interest of increased turnover on the one hand, their monopolistic restriction on the other. The promotion of linguistic uniformity is today a natural result of the interests of publishers and writers, as opposed to the earlier common tendency to maintain linguistic peculiarities or even for secret languages to be built up.

Conditions

Both the extent and the methods of regulation and exclusion in relation to outsiders may vary widely, so that the transition from a state of openness to one of regulation and closure is fluid. Various conditions of participation may be laid down; qualifying tests, a period of probation, requirement of possession of a share which can be purchased under certain conditions, election of new members by ballot, membership or eligibility by birth or by achievements open to anyone. Finally, in case of closure and the appropriation of rights within the group, membership may be dependent on the acquisition of an appropriated right. There is a wide variety of different degrees of closure and of conditions of participation. Thus "regulation" and "closure" are relative concepts. There are all manner of fluid shadings as between an exclusive club, a theatrical audience the members of which have purchased tickets, and a party rally to which the largest possible number has been urged to come; similarly, from a church service open to the general public through the rituals to a restricted sect for the mysteries of a secret cult.

Closed Relationship

Motives of Closed Relationship

The principal *motives* for closure of a relationship are: (A) The maintenance of quality, which is often combined with the interest in prestige and the consequent opportunities to enjoy honor, and even profit. Examples are communities of ascetics, monastic orders, especially, for instance, the Indian mendicant communities, religious sects like the Puritans, warrior bands, of retainers and other functionaries, citizen communities as in the Greek states, craft guilds; (B) orientation to the scarcity of "consumption opportunity." Examples are monopolies of consumption, the most developed form of which is a self-subsistent village community; (C) orientation to the scarcity of "profit-making opportunities." This is found in trade monopolies such as the guilds, the ancient monopolies of fishing rights, and so on. Usually motive in prestige is combined with the scarcity of consumption or profit-making. There are various ways in which it is possible for a closed social relationship to guarantee its monopolized opportunity for the parties. Such advantages may be left free to competitive struggle within the group; they may be regulated or rationed in amount and kind, or they may be *appropriated* by individuals or groups on a permanent basis and become more or less inalienable. The last is a case of closure within as well as against outsiders.

Terms of Closed Relationship

The probability of appropriation will be called "rights." As conditioned by the relevant order, appropriation may be for the benefit of the members of particular community or society (for instance, household community), or for the benefit of individuals. In the latter case, the individual may enjoy one's rights on a purely personal basis or in such a way that in case of one's death one or more other persons related to the holder of the right by birth (kinship). Or the rights may pass to one or more individuals specifically designated by the holder (hereditary appropriation). Finally, it may be that the holder is more or less fully empowered to alienate one's rights by voluntary agreement, either to other specific persons or to anyone he or she chooses. This is *alienable* appropriation. A party to a closed social relationship will be called a "member"; in case one's participation is regulated in such a way as to guarantee one's appropriated advantages, a "privileged" member. The opportunity of appropriation is guaranteed by community or society, will be called the "inheritance"; and, if they are alienable, "free" inheritance. The seemingly useless and tedious definition of the above concepts is an example of the fact that we often neglect to think out clearly what seems to be "self-evident," because it is intuitively familiar.

Forms of Appropriation

Within a closed relationship, there are most various forms of appropriation among the members themselves and in their relations with each other may also assume the most varied forms. Thus a caste, a guild, or an association of stock exchange brokers, which is closed to outsiders, may allow to its members a perfectly free competition for all the opportunities which the group as a whole monopolizes for itself. Or it may assign every member strictly to the enjoyment of certain opportunities, such as claims over customers or particular business opportunities, for life or even on a hereditary basis. This is particularly characteristic of India. Similarly a closed group of settlers may allow its members free use of the resources of its area or may restrict them rigidly to a plot assigned to each individual household. A closed group of colonists may allow free use of the land or sanction and guarantee permanent appropriation of separate holdings. In such cases all conceivable transitional and intermediate forms can be found. Historically, the closure of eligibility to fiefs, benefices, and offices within the group, and the appropriation on the part of those enjoying them, have occurred in the most varied forms. Similarly, the establishment of rights to and possession of particular jobs on the part of workers can develop all the way from the "closed shop" to a right to a particular job. The first step in this development may be to prohibit the dismissal of a worker without the consent of the workers' representatives.

All the details must be reserved to particular studies. The most extreme form of permanent appropriation is found in cases where particular rights are guaranteed to an individual or to certain groups of them, such as households, clans, families, in such a way that it is specified in the order either that, in case of death, the rights descend to specific heirs, or that the possessor is free to transfer them to any other person at will. Such a person thereby becomes a party to the social relationship so that, when appropriation has reached this extreme within the group, it becomes to that extent an open group in relation to outsiders. This is true so long as acquisition of membership is not subject to the approval of the other, prior members.

SOLIDARY AND REPRESENTATIVE RELATIONSHIP

Definition

A social relationship by tradition or by its established order, may condition that certain types of action of some of the parties will affect to the relationship of the others. It may be that all are *responsible* for the action of anyone. In that case they will be spoken of as "solidary" relationship. Or, on the other hand, the action of certain members, the "representatives," may be responsible for the others. That is, the resulting opportunity will go to them, they will enjoy the benefits, or conversely bear the resulting losses. The representative may be conferred in accordance with the valid order in such a way (A) that it completely appropriates in all its kinds—the case of "independent" representative; or (B) it may be conferred in accordance with particular criteria, permanently or for a limited term; or (C) it may be conferred by specific acts of the members or of outside persons, again permanently or for a limited term—the case of appointed representative. There are many different conditions in which social relationships, communal or rational, develop solidary or representative relationships. In general terms, it is possible only to say that one of the most decisive is the extent to which the action of the group is oriented to violent conflict or to peaceful exchange as its end. Besides these, many special circumstances, which can only be discussed in a detailed analysis, may be of crucial importance. It is not surprising that this development is least conspicuous in groups which pursue purely ideal ends by peaceful means. Often the degree of closure against outsiders is closely connected with the development of solidary or of representative relationship. But this is by no means always the case.

Responsibility

The "responsibility" of social relationship may in practice involve both active and passive solidary relationship. All the participants may be held responsible for the action of any one just as one's self, and similarly may be entitled to receive any benefits resulting from any one's action. This responsibility may be owed to spirits or gods, that is, involve a religious orientation. Or, on the other hand, the responsibility may be owed to human beings by convention or by law. Examples by convention are blood revenge carried out against or with the help of members of the kinship, reprisals against the inhabitants of the city or the country of the offender. Examples by the law are formal punishment of relatives, members of the household or fellow-members of a community, instead of, or in addition to, the actual offender, and personal liability of members of a household or of a commercial partnership for each other's debts. Solidary relationship with god has also had very significant historical results. For instance, in the covenant of Israel with Jehovah, in early Christianity, and in the early Puritan community. On the other hand, solidary relationship may mean no more than that the members in a closed social relationship, by the traditional or established order, are equally entitled to enjoy the opportunity for provision, especially economic, which a representative has procured. In this case, representation means only in terms to the validity of its order. Examples are the "boards" of an "association," or by the representatives of a political or economic band, who are to serve the end of the band.

Solidary Relationship

Solidary relationship is typically found in the following cases: (A) in traditional community based on birth or the communal life, for example, the household and the kinship; (B) in closed relationships which maintain a monopolized position, and control over the corresponding benefits by their own power; the typical case is political bands, especially in the past, but the same situation exists today to a high degree, most strikingly in time of war; (C) in profit-making associations where the participants personally conduct the business; the type case is the business partnership; (D) in some cases, in labour associations; an example is the Artel.

Representative Relationship

Representative relationship is most frequently found in associations devoted to specific purposes and in organized bands, especially when they gather and administrate the participants according to the ability to their purpose. A representative is selected according to "criteria" such as seniority or some other rule.

COLLECTIVE BEHAVIOUR AND SOCIAL CHANGE

Collective Behaviour

A. Social change is the alteration, modification, or transformation of public policy, culture, or social institutions over time; such change usually is brought about by collective behaviour-relatively spontaneous, unstructured activity that typically violates established social norms.

B. Conditions for Collective Behaviour:

  1. Collective behaviour occurs as a result of some common influence or stimulus that produces a response from a collectivity-a relatively large number of people who mutually transcend, bypass, or subvert established institutional patterns and structures. Collectivities in which people:
     (a) Are in physical proximity to one another (such as a crowd or riot) are referred to as localized collectivities.
     (b) Are some distance apart from one another (such as rumour, fashion, and public opinion) are referred to as dispersed collectivities.
  2. Major factors that contribute to the likelihood that collective behaviour will occur are:
     (a) Structural factors that increase the chances of people responding in a particular way;
     (b) Timing;
     (c) A breakdown in social control mechanisms and a corresponding feeling of normlessness; and
     (d) A common stimulus.

C. Dynamics of Collective Behaviour

  1. People may engage in collective behaviour when they find that their problems are not being solved through official channels; as the problem appears to

grow worse, organizational responses become more defensive and obscure.

2. People's attitudes are not always reflected in their political and social behaviour; "free riders" are people who enjoy the benefits produced by a group even though they have not helped support it.
3. People act collectively in ways they would not act singly due to:
   (a) The noise and activity around them.
   (b) A belief that it is the only way to fight those with greater power and resources.

D. *Distinctions Regarding Collective Behaviour*

1. People engaging in collective behaviour may be a:
   (a) Crowd-a relatively large number of people who are in one another's immediate face-to-face presence; or
   (b) Mass-a number of people who share an interest in a specific idea or issue but who are not in one another's immediate physical vicinity.
2. Collective behaviour also may be distinguished by the dominant emotion expressed (*e.g.*, fear, hostility, joy, grief, disgust, surprise, or shame).

E. *Types of Crowd Behaviour*

1. Herbert Blumer divided crowds into four categories:
   (a) Casual crowds-relatively large gatherings of people who happen to be in the same place at the same time; if they interact at all, it is only briefly.
   (b) Conventional crowds-people who specifically come together for a scheduled event and thus share a common focus (*e.g.*, religious services, graduation ceremonies, and college lectures). Since these events occur regularly, interaction is much more likely.

(c) Expressive crowds-people releasing their pent-up emotions in conjunction with others who experience similar emotions (*e.g.*, religious revival services, mourning crowds, and celebrating crowds). d. Acting crowds-collectivities so intensely focused on a specific purpose or object that they may erupt into violent or destructive behaviour. Examples:

(i) A mob-a highly emotional crowd whose members engage in, or are ready to engage in, violence against a specific target-a person, a category of people, or physical property.

(ii) A riot-violent crowd behaviour fuelled by deep-seated emotions but not directed at a specific target.

(iii) A panic-a form of crowd behaviour that occurs when a large number of people react with strong emotions and self-destructive behaviour to a real or perceived threat.

2. To these four types of crowds, Clark McPhail and Ronald T. Wohlstein added protest crowds-crowds that engage in activities intended to achieve specific political goals (*e.g.*, sit-ins, marches, boycotts, and strikes).

(i) Protest crowds sometimes take the form of civil disobedience-nonviolent action that seeks to change a policy or law by refusing to comply with it.

(2) At the grassroots level, protests often are seen as the only way to call attention to problems or demand social change.

G. *Explanations of Crowd Behaviour*

1. According to contagion theory, people are more likely to engage in antisocial behaviour in a crowd

because they are anonymous and feel invulnerable; Gustave Le Bon argued that feelings of fear and hate are contagious in crowds because people experience a decline in personal responsibility.

2. According to Robert Park, social unrest is transmitted by a process of circular reaction-the interactive communication between persons in such a way that the discontent of one person is communicated to another who, in turn, reflects the discontent back to the first person.
3. Convergence theory focuses on the shared emotions, goals, and beliefs many people bring to crowd behaviour.
   (a) From this perspective, people with similar attributes find a collectivity of like-minded persons with whom they can release their underlying personal tendencies.
   (b) Although people may reveal their "true selves" in crowds, their behaviour is not irrational; it is highly predictable to those who share similar emotions or beliefs.
4. According to Ralph Turner and Lewis Killian's emergent norm theory, crowds develop their own definition of the situation and establish norms for behaviour that fits the occasion.
   (a) Emergent norms occur when people define a new situation as highly unusual or see a long-standing situation in a new light.
   (b) Some emergent norms are permissive-they give people a shared conviction that they may disregard ordinary rules such as waiting in line.
   (c) Emergent norm theory points out that crowds are not irrational; new norms are developed in a rational way to fit the needs of the immediate situation.

H. Mass behaviour is collective behaviour that takes place when people (who often are geographically separated from one another) respond to the same event in much the same way. The most frequent types of mass behaviour are:

1. Rumours (unsubstantiated reports on an issue or subject) and gossip (rumours about the personal lives of individuals).
   (a) While rumours may spread through an assembled collectivity, they also may be transmitted among people who are dispersed geographically.
   (b) Starting out with a kernel of truth, as rumours spread they may be modified to serve the interests of those repeating them. Rumours thrive when tensions are high and little authentic information is available on an issue of great concern.
   (c) People are willing to give rumours credence when no offsetting information is available. Once rumours begin to circulate, they seldom stop unless compelling information comes to the forefront that either proves the rumour false or makes it obsolete.
   (d) Mass hysteria is a form of dispersed collective behaviour that occurs when a large number of people react with strong emotions and self-destructive behaviour to a real or perceived threat; many sociologists believe this behaviour is best described as a panic with a dispersed audience (*e.g.*, the radio broadcast of H.G. Wells's *The War of the Worlds*).

2. *Fads and Fashions*
   (a) A fad is a temporary but widely copied activity enthusiastically followed by large numbers of people.
   (b) Fashion is a currently valued style of behaviour, thinking, or appearance. Fashion also applies to art, music, drama, literature, architecture, interior design, and automobiles, among other things.
      (i) According to Georg Simmel, members of the lower classes emulate the fashions of the upper class. As fashions descend the status hierarchy, they are watered down and "vulgarized" so that they no longer are recognizable to members of the upper class, who then regard them as unfashionable.
      (ii) Thorstein Veblen asserted that fashion served mainly to institutionalize conspicuous consumption among the wealthy.
      (iii) Pierre Bourdieu suggested that "matters of taste," including fashion sensibility, constitute a large share of the "cultural capital" possessed by members of the dominant class.
      (iv) According to Herbert Blumer, "collective selection" best explains fashion: people in the middle and lower classes follow fashion because it is "fashion," not because they seek to emulate elites.
4. Public opinion consists of the attitudes and beliefs communicated by ordinary citizens to decision makers (as measured through polls and surveys based on interviews and questionnaires).

(a) Even on a single topic, public opinion will vary widely based on characteristics such as race, ethnicity, religion, and region of the country, urban or rural residence, social class, education level, gender, and age.

(b) Scholars who examine public opinion are interested in the extent to which the public's attitudes are communicated to decision makers, and what effect (if any) public opinion has on policymaking.

(c) As the masses attempt to influence elites and vice versa, a two-way process occurs with the dissemination of propaganda-information provided by individuals or groups that have a vested interest in furthering their own cause or damaging an opposing one.

THEORIES OF CROWD PSYCHOLOGY

Classical Theories

The main idea of Sigmund Freud's crowd behaviour theory is that people who are in a crowd act differently towards people who are thinking individually. His explanation is that the minds of the group would merge together to form a way of thinking which meant that each other's enthusiasm would be doubled and you would be less aware of what the true nature of your doings and more aware of the crowd behaviour and be swept up in the moment.

Crowds foster anonymity and sometimes generate emotion has become somewhat of a cliché. "The madding crowd" does not take on a life of its own, apart from the thoughts and intentions of members the crowd was composed of many small groups of people mostly trying to help each other. Crowds do not have a soul of their own, Rather, individuals identify themselves to their leaders through their own "ideal ego"

Convergence Theory

Convergence theory holds that crowd behaviour is not a product of the crowd itself, but is carried into the crowd by particular individuals. Thus, crowds amount to a convergence of like-minded individuals. In other words, while contagion theory states that crowds cause people to act in a certain way, convergence theory says the opposite: that people who wish to act in a certain way come together to form crowds.

Convergence theory claims that crowd behaviour as such is not irrational; rather, people in crowds express existing beliefs and values so that the mob reaction is the rational product of widespread popular feeling.

Emergent-Norm Theory

Ralph Turner and *Lewis Killian*—social behaviour is never entirely predictable, but neither are crowds as irrational. If similar interests may draw people together, distinctive patterns of behaviour may emerge in the crowd itself. Crowds begin as collectivities, acting, and protest crowds—norms may be vague and changing as when, say, one person at a rock concert holds up a lit cigarette lighter to signal praise for the performers, and other follow suit. In short, people in crowds make their own rules as they go along.

Decision-making, then, plays a major role in crowd behaviour, although casual observers of a crowd may not realize it. Crowd behaviour reflects the desires of participants, but it is also guided by norms that emerge as the situation unfolds. Emergent-norm theory points out that people in a crowd take on different roles. Some step forward as leaders; others become lieutenants, rank-and-file followers, inactive bystanders or even opponents. Each Member in the crowd plays a significant role.

Mob Rule

Ochlocracy is government by mob or a mass of people, or the intimidation of constitutional authorities. In English, the word mobocracy is sometimes used as a synonym. As a pejorative for majoritarianism, it's akin to the Latin phrase mobile vulgus meaning "the easily moveable crowd."

Chapter 4

Sociology of Mob

Both sociology and psychology deal with the causes of peoples' actions. Social psychology deals with the interaction of individuals so it looks like a very near neighbour of sociology. But sociology is the inverse of social psychology: while social psychology treats social groups as the sum of the interactions of the individuals within them, sociology treats individuals as the sum of the social groups in which they have grown up and live.

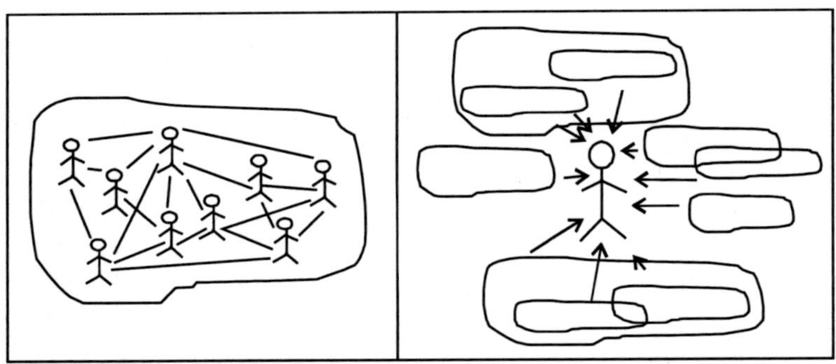

SOCIAL PYSCHOLOGY
The 'doud' of vocal collectivity is made up of interacting individuals

SOCIOLOGY
Individuals are made from the 'doudi' in which they are locally embedded

Natural languages and their speakers are social collectivities. Sociology, tries to critically analyse how people organise and participate in groups, collectivities or societies.

In sociology, a group is usually defined as a collection of humans or animals, who share certain characteristics, interact with one another, accept expectations and obligations as members of the group, and share a common identity. Using this definition, society can appear as a large group.

While an aggregate comprises merely a number of individuals, a group in sociology exhibits cohesiveness to a larger degree. Characteristics that members in the group may share include interests, values, ethnic/linguistic background, and kinship ties.

TYPES OF GROUPS

Primary groups consist of small groups with intimate, kin-based relationships: families, for example. They commonly last for years. They are small and display face to face interaction.

Secondary groups, in contrast to primary groups, are large groups whose relationships are formal and institutional. Some of them may last for years but some may disband after a short lifetime. The formation of primary groups happens within secondary groups.

Individuals almost universally have a bond toward what are known as "*Reference Groups*". These are groups to which the individual conceptually relates him/herself, and from which he/she adopts goals and values as a part of his/her self identity.

Muzafer Sherif (1916-1982) formulated a more technical definition with the following elements:

A social unit consisting of a number of individuals interacting with each other with respect to:

1. Common motives and goals;
2. An accepted division of labour, *i.e.* roles,
3. Established status (social rank, dominance) relationships;

4. Accepted norms and values with reference to matters relevant to the group;
5. Development of accepted sanctions (praise and punishment) if and when norms were respected or violated.

This definition is long and complex, but it is also precise. It succeeds at providing the researcher with the tools required to answer three important questions:

1. "How is a group formed?"
2. "How does a group function?"
3. "How does one describe those social interactions that occur on the way to forming a group?"

THE MICRO-POLITICS

Mostly we don't experience life as a series of group pressures, we experience it as a series of wise or stupid, brilliant or dumb, and good or evil acts. There is very often a tension between explaining an act as at the level of the group and explaining it at the level of the individual. This tension comes up over and over again.

For example, discussions of crime and punishment are torn between the idea that the criminal is a product of his or her social group and the idea that a criminal act is a matter of personal responsibility; the political wind blows back and forth and different groups try to make different kinds of political capital out of it.

Conflict

Sociology is also strongly interested in social conflict. Why are some societies so conflict-ridden, and what kinds of social divisions lie behind such conflicts. Why is it that difference of ethnicity, religion and gender are the basis of major conflict in some societies, and yet are the source of much less tension in other societies. Who decides what 'bad' conflict is and what is 'good'?

Orientation to Others-Social Action

Social action, which includes both failure to act and passive acceptance, may be oriented to the past, present, or expected future behaviour of others. Thus it may be motivated by revenge for a past attack, defense against present, or measures of defense against future aggression. The "others" may be known individual persons, or may constitute unknown individuals.

Mass-Conditioned Action

Social action is not identical either with the *similar* actions of many persons or with action *influenced* by other persons. Thus, if at the beginning of a shower a number of people on the street put up their umbrellas at the same time, this would not ordinarily be a case of action mutually oriented to that of each other, but rather of all reacting in the same way to the like need of protection from the rain. It is well known that the actions of the individual are strongly influenced by the mere fact that he or she is a member of a "mass" confined within a limited space. Thus, it will be called "mass-*conditioned*" action. It is also possible for large numbers, though dispersed, to be influenced simultaneously or successively by a source of influence operating similarly on all the individuals, as by means of the press. Here also the behaviour of an individual is influenced by the fact that he or she is felt of being a member of the mass. Some types of reaction are only made possible by the mere fact that the individual acts as part of a mass. Orientation to others becomes more difficult under these conditions. Hence it is possible that a particular event or mode of human behaviour can give rise to the most diverse kinds of sentiment—joy, anger, enthusiasm, despair, and passions of all sorts—in a mass situation which would not occur at all or not nearly so readily if the individual were alone. But for this to happen there need not, at least in many cases, be any *meaningful* relation between the behaviour of the individual and the fact that he or she is a member of a mass.

Imitation

But furthermore, mere "imitation" of the action of others will not be considered a case of specifically social action if it is purely reactive so that there is no meaningful orientation to the actor imitated. The mere fact that a person is found to employ some apparently useful procedure which he or she learned from someone else does not, however, constitute, in the present sense, social action. Such action is not oriented to the behaviour of the other person, but the actor has, through observing the other, become acquainted with certain objective; and it is these to which one's action is oriented. One's action is then causally conditioned by the action of others, but not meaningfully. On the other hand, if the action of others is imitated because it is "fashionable" or traditional or exemplary, or lends social honor, or on similar grounds, it is meaningfully oriented either to the behaviour of the source of imitation or of third persons or of both. There are of course all manner of transitional cases between the two types of imitation.

Borderline

Phenomena, mass-conditioned action and imitation, stand on the fluid borderline of social action. The reason for the fluidness of the line lies in the fact that both the orientation to the behaviour of others and its meaning to the actor's own oneself, are by no means always clear or conscious, but often unconscious. Mere "influence" and meaningful "orientation" cannot therefore always be clearly differentiated. But conceptually it is essential to distinguish them, even though merely "reactive" imitation may well have a degree of sociological importance at least equal to that of the type which can be called social action in the strict sense.

Types of Social Action

Social action, like other forms of action, may be classified in the following four types of orientation:

- Traditional,
- Affectual,
- Value-rational and
- End-rational.

(1) Traditional action is conditioned by accustomed habituation. (2) *Affectual*, especially *emotional,* action is conditioned by affection and states of emotion. (3) *Value-rational* action orients to purely a certain behaviour for its own sake through the conscious belief in its unconditional value (ethical, atheistic, religious or other meaningful value). Such value does not depend on its result. (4) *End-rational* action strives for the actor's own ends through expectations of the behaviour of other person or objects in the external situation. This action makes use of these expectations as "conditions" or "means" for rationally calculated ends.

Traditional Action

Strictly traditional behaviour lies very close to the borderline of what can be called "meaningfully" oriented action; it is very often a matter of automatic reaction to a course of behaviour which has been habitually accustomed. The great bulks of all everyday action to which people have become habitually accustomed approaches this type.

Affectual Action

Purely affectual behaviour also stands on the borderline of what can be considered "meaningfully" oriented action, and often it, too, goes over the line. It may, for instance, consist in an uncontrolled reaction to some exceptional stimulus. It is called sublimation when affectually conditioned action occurs in the form of conscious release of emotional tension. Sublimation leads to usually, though not always, the road to "value-rational" or end-rational action, or the combination of both.

Value-rational Action

Value-rational orientation of action is distinguished from the affectual type by clearly self-conscious and *consistently* planned orientation to its ultimate values. At the same time the two types have a common element, namely that the meaning of the action does not depend on its result, but on the specific attitude of action for its own sake. Affectual action is oriented to the satisfaction of a direct emotion such as revenge, sensuality, devotion, and contemplative bliss, or, finally, toward discharging emotional tensions regardless of how mass-conditioned or sublimed they may be.

On the other hand, pure value-rational action without considering possible cost of its consequence, orients to duty, dignity, beauty, religious call, piety, or "cause" no matter in what it consists. For the purposes of our terminology, value-rational action always involves "commands" or "demands" to the fulfillment of which the actor believes as duty. We will attribute an action to value-rational only where human action is motivated by the fulfillment of such unconditional demands. Value-rational action is empirically the case in widely varying degrees, but for the most part only to a relatively slight extent. Nevertheless, this action is observable enough to formulate as a distinct type; though it may be remarked that there is no intention here of attempting to formulate in any sense an exhaustive classification of types of action.

Prejudice

Prejudice is the negative attitudes towards the members of some social group on their membership in this group.

The Conflict Theory proposes that prejudice stems at least in part from competition between social groups over valued commodities or opportunities.

Social Categorization states the tendency to divide the social world into two distinct categories 'us' and 'them'.

Stereotypes are the cognitive frame works suggesting that all members of specific social groups share certain characteristics.

The Psychology of Prejudice: Ingroup Love or Outgroup Hate?

Ingroups and Outgroups

Groups exist by virtue of there being out-groups. For a collection of people to be a group there must, logically, be other people who are not in the group (a diffuse non-ingroup, *e.g.*, academics vs. non-academics) or people who are in a specific out-group (*e.g.*, academics vs. politicians). In this sense, social groups are categories of people; and just like other categories, a social category acquires its meaning by contrast with other categories. The social world is patterned by social discontinuities that marks the boundaries of social groups in terms of perceived and/or actual differences in what people think, feel, and do.

Definition: Prejudice is a baseless and usually negative attitude toward members of a group. Common features of prejudice include negative feelings, stereotyped beliefs, and a tendency to discriminate against members of the group. In its original use, the word *prejudice* refers to prejudgement: *i.e.*

making a decision before becoming aware of the relevant facts of a case.

Allport (1954) recognized that attachment to one's in groups does not necessarily require hostility toward outgroups. Yet the prevailing approach to the study of ethnocentrism, in group bias, and prejudice presumes that in group love and outgroup hate are reciprocally related.

Allport postulates that ingroups are "psychologically primary," in the sense that familiarity, attachment, and preference for one's ingroups come prior to development of attitudes toward specific outgroups. Further, Allport recognized that preferential positivity toward ingroups does not necessarily imply negativity or hostility toward outgroups. Indeed, ingroup love can be compatible with a range of attitudes toward corresponding outgroups, including mild positivity, indifference, disdain, or hatred.

Allport's s insights about the nature of ingroup-outgroup attitudes stand in contrast to the inherited wisdom represented in Sumner's (1906) original treatment of the concepts of ethnocentrism, ingroups, and outgroups. Like Allport, Sumner defined ethnocentrism in terms of positive sentiments toward the ingroup: pride, loyalty, and perceived superiority. However, Sumner also believed that these positive sentiments toward the ingroup were directly correlated with contempt, hatred, and hostility toward outgroups. As he put it:

The relation of comradeship and peace in the we-group and that of hostility and war towards others-groups are correlative to each other. The exigencies of war with outsiders are what make peace inside.... Loyalty to the group, sacrifice for it, hatred and contempt for outsiders, brotherhood within, warlikeness without—all grow together, common products of the same situation. (Sumner, 1906, P. 12)

Prejudice refers to what people believe is true. An example of cognitive prejudice might be found, for example, adherence to a particular metaphysical or methodological philosophy to the exclusion of other philosophies that may offer a more complete theoretical explanation.

Affective Prejudice refers to what people like and dislike. An example of affective prejudice might be found, for example, in attitudes toward members of particular classes such as race, ethnicity, national origin, or creed.

Co native Prejudice refers to how people are inclined to behave. Co native prejudice is regarded as an attitude because people don't act on their feelings. An example of co native prejudice might be found in expressions of what should be done if the opportunity presented itself. These three types of prejudice are correlated, but all need not be present in a particular individual.

Discrimination is a behaviour (an action), with reference to unequal treatment of people because they are members of a particular group. Farley also classified discrimination into three categories.

Personal/Individual Discrimination is directed toward a specific individual and refers to any act that leads to unequal treatment because of the individual's real or perceived group membership.

Legal Discrimination refers to "unequal treatment, on the grounds of group membership, that is upheld by law." Apartheid is an example of legal discrimination, as are also various post-Civil war laws in the southern United States that legally disadvantaged negros with respect to property rights, employment rights and the exercise of constitutional rights.

Institutional Discrimination refers to unequal treatment that is entrenched in basic social institutions resulting in advantaging one group over another. The Indian caste system is an historical example of institutional discrimination. As with prejudice generally, these three types of discrimination are correlated and may be found to varying degrees in individuals and society at large. Many forms of discrimination based upon prejudice are outwardly unacceptable in most societies.

PERSUASION & INFLUENCE

We are inclined to believe those we do not know, because they have never deceived us.

—Samuel Johnson (1709-1784)

As Plato observed, persuasion is the key to power.

- In his *Rhetoric*, Aristotle distinguished three factors influencing communication:
- Ethos, involving characteristics of the speaker which enhance the persuasive impact of the speech;
- Pathos, the emotional reactions in the audience which facilitate or inhibit the persuasive impact of the speech; and
- Logos, the argument's logic within the message itself.

Perhaps at least one other dimension needs to be taken into account based on lessons learned from 20th century refinements of the arts "brainwashing," and altering the minds of those to be persuaded.

Media

Most of what we "know" is actually second-hand knowledge, information and insight that we obtain from others. Further, *how* we come to know anything is grasped in terms of symbols, and the meaning content of symbols is, in large part, determined by the *form* in which they are socially shared. Because of technological innovations, such as the inventions of television and computers, these symbolic forms are being fundamentally altered. It is for this reason that Marshall McLuhan (1967) argued that the medium is the message; what's important is not, for instance, what people watch on television but rather that they watch it. Given their symbolic dependency, changes in both social systems and self-systems have resulted.

Communications determinists argue that culture and institutions are only subsystems of communications technology. Harold Innis (1951), for instance, observed how all mediums of communication are biased in terms of their control of time or space. Media that are durable and difficult to transport—such as the clay tablets upon which ancient Babylonians etched their cuneiform or the stone columns on which ancient Egyptians affixed their hieroglyphics—are *time-binding* or time-biased. Media that are light, easily transportable, but less durable—such as television waves, telephone messages, or the thin parchment carried by pony express riders in the 1860s—are said to be *space-binding*. Innis argued that space-binding media encourage the growth of the state, the military and decentralized institutions. Time-binding media, on the other hand, foster concern with history and tradition, and favor the growth of religion and hierarchical organizations.

Reputations

The notion of reputation sheds further light on both how situations are framed and the social bases of identity. A reputation involves others' shared image of an individual and its associated esteem. Reputations, whether good or bad or deserved or not, filter how others interpret one's self presentations.

Hate Groups

Hatred toward members of perceived out-groups is a powerful source of in-group solidarities. Times of economic and political uncertainty spawn various hate groups, attracting individuals, often young adults, who feel left out of the mainstream and who feel to be in possession of some absolute truth. While other countries may have their Fundamentalist religious zealots, in the United States such extremism is more often bred by economics and politics feel to be in possession of some absolute truth. While other countries may have their Fundamentalist religious zealots, in the United States such extremism is more often bred by economics and politics.

Chapter 5

Bureaucracy

Glorification of vigilante justice as being meted out to criminals in Bihar. persons killed in Vaishali might not actually be thieves. Suppose they really do not turn out to be thieves after thorough investigations, can one imagine what kind of injustice has been meted to them in the name of instant justice?

There is a serious crisis there and it requires tough and swift administrative measures to restore the faith of people in the system. Our anger should be against law and order machinery and elected representatives. That too within the democratic means.

BUREAUCRACIES

The bureaucratic model of organization remains the most universal organizational form in government, business, education, and religion. A *bureaucracy* is an organizational model characterized by a hierarchy of authority, a clear division of labour, explicit rules and procedures, and impersonality in personnel matters.

When we think of a bureaucracy, we may think of "buck-passing," such as occurs when we are directed from one office to the next without receiving an answer to our question or a solution to our problem. We also may view a bureaucracy in terms of "red tape" because of the situations in which there is so much paperwork and so many incomprehensible rules that no one really understands what to do. However, the bureaucracy was originally not intended to be this way; it was seen as a way to make organizations *more* productive and efficient.

Getman sociologist Max Weber (1968/1922) was interested in the historical trend toward bureaucratization that accelerated during the Industrial Revolution. To Weber, the bureaucracy was the most "rational" and efficient means of attaining organizational goals because it contributed to

coordination and control. According to Weber, rituality is the process by which traditional methods of social organization, characterized by informality and spontaneity, are gradually replaced by efficiently administered forma! rules and procedures. This process can be seen in all aspects of our lives, from small colleges with perhaps a thousand students to multinational corporations employing many thousands of workers worldwide. In his study of bureaucracies, Weber relied on middle-type analysis, which he adapted from the field of economics. An ideal type is an abstract model that describes the recurring characteris-estics of some phenomenon (such as bureaucracy). To develop this ideal type, Weber abstracted the most characteristic bureaucratic aspects of religious, educational, political, and business organization. For example, to develop an ideal type for bureaucracy in higher education, you would need to include the relationships among governing bodies (such as boards of regents or trustees), administrators, faculty, staff, and students. You would also have to include the rules and policies that govern the school's activities (such as admissions criteria, grading policies, and graduation requirements). Although no two schools would have exactly the same criteria, the ideal-type constructs would be quite similar. Weber acknowledged that no existing organization would exactly fit his ideal type of bureaucracy (Blau and Meyer, 1987).

Ideal Characteristics of Bureaucracy

Weber set forth several ideal-type charactetistics of bureaucratic organizations. Although bureaucratic realities often differ from these ideal charactetistics, Leber's model highlights the organizational efficiency and productivity that bureaucracies strive for. The model has been criticized for not taking into account informal networks (Roethlisberger and Dickson, 1939; Blau and Meyer, 1987). However, it is not surprising that these patterns are largely ignored in Weber's theory of bureaucracy; he constructed an idealized model that deliberately overlooked imperfections and unintended outcomes (Blau and Meyer, 1987).

Division of Labour: Bureaucratic organizations are characterized by specialization, and each member has a specific status with certain assigned tasks to fulfill. This division of labour requires the employment of specialized experts who are responsible for the effective performance of their duties.

Hierarchy of Authority: In the sense that Weber described hierarchy of authority, or chain command, it includes each lower office being under the control and supervision of a higher one. Sociologist Charles Perrow (1986) has noted that all groups with a division of labour are hierarchies, structured. Although the chain of command is not always followed, "in a crunch, the chain is there for those higher up to use it." Authority that is distributed hierarchically takes the form of a pyramid; those few individuals at the top have more power and exercise more control than do the many at the lower levels. Hierarchy inevitably influences social interaction. Those who are lower in the hierarchy report to (and often take orders from) those above them in the organizational pyramid. Persons at the upper levels are responsible not only for their own actions but also for those of the individuals they supervise. Hierarchy has been described as a graded system of interpersonal relationships, a society of unequal in which scarce rewards become even more scarce further down the hierarchy (Perthus, 1978).

Rules and Regulations: Weber asserted that rules and regulations establish authority within an organization. These rules are typically standardized and provided to members in the written format. In theory, written rules and regulations offer clear-cut standards for determining satisfactory performance. They also provide continuity so that each new member does not have to reinvent the necessary rules and regulations.

Qualification-Based Employment: Bureaucracies them staff members and professional employees based on specific qualifications. Favoritism, family connections, and other subjective factors not relevance on organizational efficiency are not acceptable criteria for employment. Individual performance is evaluated against specific standards, and promotions are based on merit as spelled out in personnel policies.

Impersonality: A detached approach should prevail toward clients so that personal feelings do not interfere with organizational decisions. Officials must interact with subordinates based on their official status, not on their personal feelings about them.

Informal Structure in Bureaucracies: When we look at an organizational chatt, the official, formal structure of a bureaucracy is readily apparent. In practice, however, a bureaucracy has patterns of activities and interactions that cannot be accounted for by its organizational chart. These have been referred to as bureaucracy's *other face* (Page, 1946). An organization's informal structure is composed of those aspects of participants' day-to-day activities and interactions that ignore, bypass, or do not correspond with the official rules and procedures of the bureaucracy. An example is an informal "grapevine" that spreads information (with varying degrees of accuracy) much faster than do official channels of communication, which tend to be slow and unresponsive. The informal structure has also been referred to as work culture and includes the ideology and practices of workers on the job. It is the "informal, customary values and rules [that] mediate the formal authority structure of the workplace and distance workers from its impact" (Benson, 1983: 185). Workers create this work culture in order to confront, resist, or adapt to the constraints of their jobs, as well as to guide and interpret social relations on the job (Zavella, 1987).

POSITIVE AND NEGATIVE ASPECTS OF INFORMAL STRUCTURE

Is informal structure good or bad? Should it be controlled or encouraged? Two schools of thought have emerged with regard to these questions. One approach emphasizes control (or eradication) of informal groups; the other suggests that they should be nurtured. Traditional management theories are based on the assumption that people are basically lazy and motivated by greed. Consequently, informal groups must be controlled (or eliminated) in order to ensure greater worker productivity.

The other school of thought asserts that organizations should foster informal groups that permit people to work more efficiently toward organizational goals. Chester Barnard (1938), an early organizational theorist, focused on the functional aspects of informal groups. He suggested that organizations are cooperative systems in which informal groups "oil the wheels" by providing understanding and motivation for participants. In other words, informal networks serve as a means of communication and cohesion among individuals, as well as protecting the integrity of the individual (Barnard, 1938; Perrow, 1986).

More-recent studies have confirmed the importance of informal networks in bureaucracies. Some scholars have argued that women and people of receive color receive fairer treatment in larger bureaucracies than they do in smaller organizations, but others have stressed that they may be categorically *excluded* from networks that are important for survival and advancement in the organization (Kanter, 1993; South *et al.*, 1982; Benokraitis and Feagin, 1986; Feagm, 1991). A woman firefighter, in New York City describes how detrimental and even hazardous, it is for workers to be excluded from such informal networks because of race/ethnicity, gender, or other attributes;

I had sort of a "Pollyanna" view of how long it would take before women were really accepted in these nontraditional very male-dominated jobs [such as being a firefighter]. One always thinks that women prove that we

can do the job well, people will just accept us and we'll all fit in... [However,] I went to a firehouse where the men refused to eat with me. They would not talk to me. On one occasion my protective gear had been tampered with. It was always a big question as to whether fact you have anyone there to hack you up when you needed them. (PBS, 1992b)

White women and people of color who are employed in positions traditionally held by white men such as firefighters, police officers, and factory workers) often experience categorical exclusion from the informal structure. Not only do they lack of informal network to "grease the wheels"; they may also be harassed and endangered by the it co-workers. In sum, the informal structure is critical for employees—whether they ate allowed participating or not.

Shortcomings of Bureaucracies

As noted previously, Weber's description of bureaucracy was intentionally an abstract, idealized model of a rationally organized institution. However, the very characteristics that make up this 'rational" model have a dark side that has frequently given this type of organization a bad name (*see* Figure 5.1). Three of the major problems of bureaucracies are (1) inefficiency and rigidity, (2) resistance to change, and (3) perpetuation of race, class, and gender inequalities (see Blau and Meyer, 1987).

Inefficiency and Rigidity Bureaucracies experience inefficiency and rigidity at both the upper and lower levels of the organization. The self-protective behaviour of officials at the top may render the organization inefficient. One type of self-protective behaviour is the monopolization of information in order to maintain control over subordinates and outsiders. Information is a valuable commodity in organizations. Theoretically, budgets and long-range plans are based on relevant information, and decisions are made based on the best available data. However, those in positions of authority guard information because it is a source of power for them—others cannot "second-guess" their decisions without access to relevant (and often "confidential") information (Blau and Meyer, 1987).

This information blockage is intensified by the hierarchical arrangement of officials and workers. Those at the top tend to use their power and authority to monopolize information, and they also fail to communicate with workers at the lower levels. As a result, officials are often unaware of potential problems facing the organization and of high levels of worker frustration. Meanwhile, those at the bottom of the structure hide their mistakes from supervisors, a practice that may ultimately result in disaster for the organization.

Policies and procedures also contribute to inefficiency and rigidity. Sociologists Peter M. Blau and Marshall W. Meyer (1987) have suggested that bureaucratic regulations are similar to bridges and buildings in that they are designed to withstand far greater stresses than they will ever experience. Accordingly, bureaucratic regulations are written in far greater detail than is necessary, in order to ensure that almost all conceivable situations are covered. *Qaal displacement* occurs when the rules become an end in themselves rather than a means-to-an-end, and organizational survival becomes more important than achievement of goals (Merton, 1968). Administrators tend to overconform to the rules because their expertise is knowledge of the regulations, and they are paid to enforce them. They also fear that if they bend the rules for one person, they may be accused of violating the norm of impersonality and engaging in favoritism (Blau and Meyer, 1987).

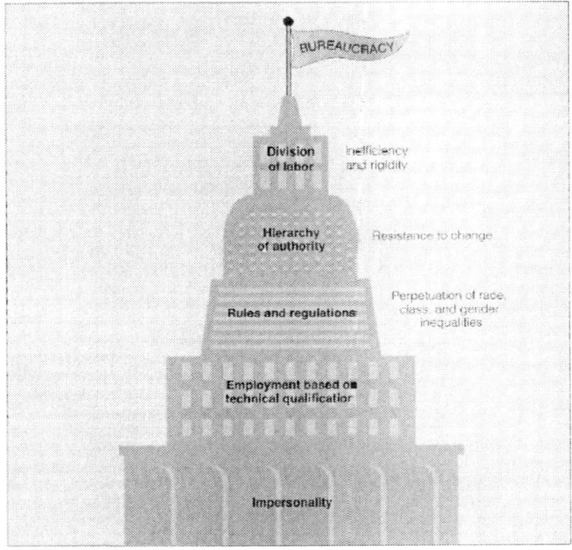

The very characteristics that define Weber's bureaucracy can create or exacerbate the problems that many people associate with this type of organization, Can apply this model to an organization which you are familiar?

Figure 5.1: Characteristics and Effects of Bureaucracy

Inefficiency and rigidity occur at die lower levels of the organization as well. Workers often engage in *ritualism;* that is, they become most concerned with "going through the motions" and "following the tules." According to Robert Merton (1968), the term *bureaucratic personality* describes those workers who are more concerned with following correct procedures than they are with getting the job done correctly. Such workers are usually able to handle routine situations effectively but are frequently incapable of handling a unique problem or an emergency. Thorstein Veblen (1967/1899) used the term *trained incapacity* to characterize situations in which workers have become so highly specialized, or have been given such fragmented jobs to do, that they are unable to come up with creative solutions to problems. Workers who have reached this point also tend to experience bureaucratic alienation—they really do not care what is happening around them.

Sociologists have extensively analyzed the effects of bureaucracy on workers. Some workers may become alienated, but others may lose any identity apart from the organization. Sociologist William H. Whyte, Jr. (1957) coined the term *organization man* to identify an individual whose life | controlled by the corporation. C. Wright Mills i959a) suggested that employees become "cheer-rul robots" when they are controlled by an organization. Other scholars have argued that most workers do not reach these extremes.

Resistance to Change: Once bureaucratic organizations are created, they tend to resist change. Although the formal structure may help an organization survive during periods of crisis, it may also undermine creativity and profitability. In a study of 152 New York architectural firms, for example, the sociologist Judith R. Blau (1984) found that the same characteristics that made these firms most likely to survive an economic recession also made them the least likely to become highly profitable. Although the large, well-established firms had the corporate clients and the resources to withstand difficult economic times, their greater overhead made them less inclined than smaller firms to take risks. Some of the risky ventures taken by the smaller firms led to greater profits, but others led to bankruptcy.

Resistance to change occurs in all bureaucratic organisations, including schools, trade unions, businesses, and government agencies. This resistance not only makes bureaucracies virtually impossible to eliminate but also contributes to bureaucratic enlargement. Because of the assumed relationship between size and importance, official ten to press for larger budgets and more staff and officer space. To justify growth, administrators and managers must some up with more tasks for workers to perform.

Resistance to change may also lead to incompetence. Based on organizational policy, bureaucracies tend to promote people from within the organization. As a consequence, a person who performs satisfactorily in one position is promoted to a higher level in the organization. Eventually, people reach a level that is beyond their own knowledge, experience, and capabilities.

Perpetuation of race, class, and Gender Inequalities: Some bureaucracies perpetuate inequalities of face, class, and gender because this form of organizational structure creates a specific type of work or learning environment. This structure was typically created for middle—and upper-middle-class white men, who for many years were the predominant organizational participants.

Race and Ethnic Inequalities In a study of 209 middle class African Americans from more than a dozen cities, the sociologist Joe R. Feagin (1991) found that entry into dominant white bureaucratic organizations should not be equated with thorough integration, Instead, many have experienced an internal conflict between the bureaucratic ideals of equal opportunity and fairness and the prevailing norms of discrimination and hostility that exist in many organizations. In another study of 125 African American bankers, interviewees repeatedly indicated that they were excluded from informal communication networks and were not "in on things" in their organization. Very few had mentors or anyone else highly placed within their organizations to take an interest in furthering their careers (Irons and Moore, 1985; Cose, 1993). Other research has found that people of color are more adversely affected than dominant-group members by hierarchical bureaucratic structures.

Sociol *Class Inequalities* Like racial inequalities, social class divisions may be perpetuated in bureaucracies (Blau and Meyer, 1987). Sociologists have explored the impact of label market conditions on the kinds of jobs and wages available to workers. The theory of a "dual labour market" has been developed to explain how social class distinctions are perpetuated through different types of employment. Middle—and upper-middle-class employees are more likely to work in industries characterized by higher wages, more job security, and opportunities for advancement. By contrast, poor and working-class employees work in industries characterized by low wages, lack of job security, and few opportunities for promotion. Peter Blau and Marshall Meyer (1987: 160-161) conclude that "over time, then, organizational conditions reinforce social stratification.... Bureaucracies create profound differences in the life chances of the people working in them."

Gender Inequalities: Gender inequalities are also perpetuated in bureaucracies. Sociologist Rosabeth Moss Kanter (1993) analyzed how the power structure of bureaucratic hierarchies can negatively affect white women and people of color when they are underrepresented within an organization. In such cases, they tend to be more visible ("on display") and to feel greater pressure not to make mistakes or stand out too much. They may also find i: harder to gain credibility, particularly in management positions. As a result, they are more likely to feel isolated, to be excluded from informal networks, and to have less access to mentors and to power through alliances. By contrast, affluent white men are more likely to be seen as "belonging" to the group, and they generally have an easier time joining informal networks and finding mentors to help them get ahead (Kanter, 1993).

Gender inequality in organizations has additional consequences. People who lack opportunities for integration and advancement tend to be pessimistic and to have lower self-esteem. In addition, women working in occupations and professions traditionally dominated by men have a greater likelihood of becoming the victims of unusual harassment. Although many instances of such harassment of women are reported in the media, the media may disproportionately cover situation in which a man is the subject of the harassment discusse. Reports of overt harassment of women have come from virtually all occupational areas, including the armed forces, mines, corporate offices, universities, and factories (Lott, 1994). Whereas a specific act of sexual harassment may seem minor to those who consider it to be an "isolated situation," one blatantly discriminatory act is often combined with a number of subtle and covert behaviours as well.

Frequently, complaints of harassment are disregarded or downplayed by employers and supervisors. When officials fail to pursue grievances, they give the impression of endorsing or condoning the harassment through their inaction (Janofsky, 1993: F1, F6).

Many women do not report incidents of harassment because they fear that they may lose their job or suffer retaliation from their boss or co-workers. When harassment occurs in the workplace, women may simply quit their jobs. Those who experience harassment in college may drop a class, change majors, or transfer to another institution in order to escape the harasser. Women of color face double jeopardy in that they may experience both racial discrimination and sexual harassment (Benokraitis and Feagin, 1995).

The bottom line is that sexual or racial harassment undermines the goal of equality in the workplace and in education. Consequently, organizations must be proactive in establishing guidelines for what is considered acceptable and unacceptable behaviour. The elimination of sexual harassment must be viewed as desirable not only for moral, legal, and financial reasons but also essential for creating and maintaining a positive organizational atmosphere for all participants (see Riggs, Murrell, and Cutting, 1993).

Bureaucracy and Oligarchy

Max Weber believed that bureaucracy was a necessary evil because it achieved coordination and control and thus efficiency in administration (Blau and Meyer, 1987). However, he also believed such organizations stifle human initiative and creativity, thus producing an "iron cage." Bureaucracy also places an enormous amount of unregulated and often unperceived social power in the hands of a very few leaders. Such a situation is referred to as an oligarchy—the rule of the man by the few.

Chapter 6

Ethics and Justice

> Ethics is way of making judgments about moral behaviour of people

The Magistrate and the Angry Mob (Mob): An angry mob is threatening to wreak bloody havoc on a small and vulnerable section of the town, unless the culprit of a terrible crime is produced, convicted, and executed. The judge knows that the culprit is unknown, but does know of a certain person, a social undesirable (albeit innocent), who could be framed as the culprit, and executed in order to disperse the angry mob. The mob does not, and the judge would not want them to know, that this person would only be a scapegoat.

If one innocent person is not killed, then several innocent people will die (or be injured, terrorized). we don't have to worry about "mob rule" in the cave; we can locate the moral dilemma as occurring in a single person's thought process in each case.

There is a conflict, or apparent conflict, between two moral intuitions:

- *Utilitarian*: It is always right to perform the act which promotes less overall suffering.
- *Conservative*: It is always wrong to kill an innocent person (i.e. regardless of circumstances).

The judicial murder of an innocent man would potentially corrupt the justice system, set a bad judicial precedent, lead to further mob situations of a similar kind, if the innocence of the scapegoat is found out.

Bernard Williams, who argues against utilitarianism, seems to claim that it is not necessarily the utilitarian's answer to the moral dilemma which is wrong, but rather that the utilitarian's manner of reasoning (in order to get that answer) is morally corrupt. For the utilitarian seems to ignore, or can't take seriously, the fact that actions are performed by human beings who have commitments and projects, as wellas moral feelings which aren't necessarily utilitarian feelings. According to Williams, utilitarian reasoning is an affront to human integrity because it treats the agent as a purely causal actor—for a utilitarian, it doesn't much matter who the actor is, or who performs an action, so long as it is the right one. But this fails to take seriously the idea that our actions belong to us, that humans identify with the acts they perform just as much as (if not more than) the states of affairs brought about by those actions. That is, we are what we do. But utilitarian reasoning seems to abstract away from individuals and their identities, by claiming that the only thing that matters, or what matters ultimately, are states of affairs in the world. But it also matters, says Williams, that we are the ones who must act or refuse to act. And whether we can "live with" our actions is, or may be, more than a simple matter of adding up all the utility an action might produce.

ORIGIN OF LADY OF JUSTICE

The origin may be Themis, a Greek mythological goddess. One of the Titans, pre-Hellenic nature deities born to Uranus and Ge, she remained and advised Zeus after his purge of the old pantheon. In depictions of her, she carries the scales of justice in one hand and a sword in the other, her eyes covered. She became an oracle at Delphi, and became known as a goddess of divine justice.

A daughter of Themis and Zeus, Dike, known as a goddess of justice but not divine justice, presided over the apportionment of things among mortals, the protection of individuals and the keeping of social and political order. She carried a sword without a scale of justice. At times Dike is said to be the same (or is she confused with?) Astraea. Astraea is also said to be a daughter of Themis and Zeus and is known as a goddess of justice. Also known as daughter of Eos and Astraeus 1, her head was crowned with ears of grain and for its measure carried a balance or scale. Astraea was the last of the immortals to leave earth after the Golden Age. She has also been called a goddess of purity and innocence. She became the constellation Virgo. Dike left earth when the Race of Bronze was born.

The Egyptians honored Maat, the daughter of the sun god, Ra. She also carried a sword but without a scale of justice.

Justitia, a Roman goddess of justice, wore a blindfold. She had been depicted with sword and scales, but was not always so.

Representations of the Lady of Justice in the Western tradition occur in many places and at many times. She sometimes wears a blindfold, more so in Europe, but more often she appears without one. She usually carries a sword and scales. Almost always draped in flowing robes, mature but not old, no longer commonly known as Themis, she symbolizes the fair and equal administration of the law, without corruption, avarice, prejudice, or favor.

REPUBLIC X BY PLATO

At the beginning of the *Republic* Plato undertook to show that justice is valuable in itself, apart from any consequences, so that a just person would feel no temptation to misuse Gyges' ring. Over the course of the dialogue, Plato has argued essentially as follows:

1. Justice consists in our rational desires' possessing wisdom and ruling over our nonrational desires.
2. Wisdom is knowledge of the Good.
3. So justice involves being ruled by knowledge of the Good. (1, 2)
4. Whoever is ruled by knowledge of the Good will be filled with the most satisfying thing there is.
5. So justice involves being filled with the most satisfying thing there is. (3, 4)
6. Whoever is filled with the most satisfying thing there is will be maximally happy.
7. So justice involves being maximally happy. (5, 6)
8. Whoever is ruled by knowledge of the Good will want to reproduce goodness all around himself.
9. So justice involves wanting to reproduce goodness all around oneself. (3, 8)
10. Whoever wants to reproduce goodness all around himself will seek to benefit others.
11. So justice involves seeking to benefit others. (9, 10)
12. Justice both makes its possessor maximally happy and leads its possessor to benefit others. (7, 11)
13. In misusing Gyges' ring, one would not be seeking to benefit others.
14. Misusing Gyges' ring would involve denying oneself the state that makes its possessor maximally happy. (12, 13)

15. It is not in our self-interest to deny ourselves the state that would make us maxiomally happy.
16. It is not in our self-interest to misuse Gyges' ring. (14, 15)

Notice that this argument makes no appeal to the external rewards and penalties that just or unjust conduct might bring; Plato has focused exclusively (well, almost exclusively) on what a just or unjust soul is like in itself. But now he reminds his readers that although (in his opinion) he has shown that justice is worth having for its own sake, he thinks justice *also* is beneficial for its consequences; and in this regard he develops an account of the immortality of the soul. Recall that Socrates in the *Apology* had been agnostic about the soul's survival after death; not so Plato.

ETHICS

In ethics, of which questions about justice are a part, we similarly divide *ethics* from *metaethics*. Ethics is the assertion and justification of what is good, right, proper, or just. Metaethics concerns the nature of ethics, how ethical terms can be defined, what methods of justification are appropriate to ethics, and how we can know any of this. If our ethics insist that human rights are good, metaethics would question what we mean by a "human right" and "good" and how we know or justify this "goodness." If "natural law" is the answer, then metaethics would ask why.

Ethics guide us as to what in our behaviour is good or evil, right or wrong, just or unjust, proper or improper, moral or immoral. Of course, a painting can be good or bad, as can be a book, movie, motor, or bridge. But what distinguishes ethical from, for example, aesthetic or technological values, is that ethics carry or imply responsibility, obligation, duty. That is, we are supposed to keep our promises or support our children. Not to do so is unethical. For nonethical values, however, no such responsibility or duty is implied. If we deem a book badly written, we hardly imply that the author was obligated as a person to write a good book. The author, indeed, may have a most outstanding character, from which his badly written book would not detract at all. However, no matter how competent or skilled an author, were he to lie to us for his own gain we would immediately question his worth as a person.

In common English there are subtle differences in meaning between "morality" and "ethics." The latter seems more refined and intellectual, dealing with higher qualities. We can ignore these connotations here. In general, ethical statements are moral; prescribing what is right, wrong, good, and bad about human character, behaviour, and relationships. It is necessary to point out this property of ethical statements in order to separate them from technological, scientific, and functional oughts. "To get elected you should..." "States ought to watch over the balance of powers..." "You ought to exercise," and so on. All these are instrumental oughts toward some goal. What distinguishes them from ethics is that they lack a moral quality.

This moral quality is that of obligation and duty. One has a moral responsibility to keep promises, for example. One who fails to do so is morally lacking, deficient, or bad. To act contrary to a moral ought is to be morally questionable, subject to guilt; an object of public criticism, scorn, possibly ostracism (as with incest). Moral oughts comprise our moral attitudes, our superego

What is Justice?

Socrates stresses the fact that there is nothing more important than justice. Historical approach to justice has also been covered by Plato, Hume, and Mill.

(a) To administer justice to.

(b) The rendering to every one his due or right; just treatment; requital of desert; merited reward or punishment; that which is due to one's conduct or motives.

(c) Conformity to truth and reality in expressing opinions and in conduct; fair representation of facts respecting merit or demerit; honesty; fidelity; impartiality; as, the justice of a description or of a judgment; historical justice.

The quality of being just; conformity to the principles of righteousness and rectitude in all things; strict near the close of the twentieth century, moral and political disorders bring grave confusion about the meanings of old words. As T. S. Eliot wrote in "Burnt Norton"—Words strain,

Crack and sometimes break, under the burden,

Under the tension, slip, slide, perish,

Decay with imprecision, will not stay in place,

Will not stay still.

Shrieking voices Scolding, mocking, or merely chattering,

Always assail them.

Conspicuous among such venerable words, in our era often abused and misrepresented, is this necessary word justice.

Jeremy Taylor, in the middle of the seventeenth century, wrote that there exist two kinds of justice.

The one is commutative justice, or reciprocal justice.

The other kind is distributive justice, expressed in this passage from Romans: "Render to all their dues; tribute to whom tribute is due, custom to whom custom, fear to who fear, honor to whom honor; owe no man anything but to love one another." Upon this Taylor comments, "This justice is distinguished from the first, because the obligation depends not upon contract or express bargain, but passes upon us by some command of God, or of our superior, by nature or by grace, by piety or religion, by trust or by office, according to that commandment, 'As every man hath received the gift, so let him minister the same one to another, as good stewards of the manifold grace of God.'"

In the ancient world, the most just of men was Solon, Athens' lawgiver, poet, and hero. As Solon wrote of his reform of the Athenian constitution—

Such power I gave the people as might do, Abridged not what they had, nor lavished new; those that were great in wealth and high in place my counsel likewise kept from all disgrace. Before them both I kept my shield of might, and let not either touch the other's right.

To each class, that is, Solon gave its due, and so preserved the peace: that is social justice.

It is the influence of the Greek and Roman classics toward forming affection for justice. Until well into the nineteenth century, Cicero was studied in every decent school; and this passage from that statesman-philosopher implanted an apprehension of the nature of justice:

Law is the highest reason, implanted in nature, which commands what ought to be done and forbids the opposite. This reason, when firmly fixed and fully developed in the human mind, is law. And so they believe that law is intelligence, whose natural function it is to command right conduct and forbid wrongdoing. They think that this quality has derived its name in Greek from the idea of granting to every man his own, and in our language I believe it has been named from the idea of choosing.

Behind the phrase "to each his own" lay the beliefs that divine wisdom has conferred upon man a distinct nature; that human nature is constant; that the idea of justice is implanted in the human consciousness by a transcendent power; and that the general rule by which we endeavor to do justice is this: "to each man, the things that are his own."

Injustice, according to this doctrine, occurs when men try to undertake things, for which they are not fitted, and to claim rewards to which they are not entitled, and to deny to other men what really belongs to those other men. As Plato puts it, in The Republic, quite as an unjust man is a being whose reason, will, and appetite are at war one with another, so an unjust society is a state afflicted by "meddlesomeness, and interference, and the rising up of a part of the soul against the whole, an assertion of unlawful authority, which is made by a rebellious subject against a true prince, of whom he is the natural vassal—what is all this confusion and delusion but injustice, and intemperance and cowardice and ignorance, and every form of vice?"

Edmund Burke re-expressed this doctrine of "to each his own" when, in his Reflections on the Revolution in France, he wrote of true natural rights: "Men have a right to the fruits of their industry, and to the means of making their industry fruitful. They have a right to the acquisitions of their parents, to the nourishment and improvement of their offspring, to instruction in life, and to consolation in death.

Whatever each man can separately do, without trespassing upon others, he has a right to do for himself; and he has a right to all which society, with all its combinations of skill and force, can do in his favor."

And yet in Burke's own time, there arose a very different idea of justice, the Utilitarian concept, expounded by Jeremy Bentham. From Bentham's jurisprudence there is descended the powerful present-day school of legal thought that we call legal positivism or legal realism. Positivistic jurisprudence arose in alliance with nineteenth-century nationalism and with scientific mechanism and materialism. To the legal positivist or realist, laws are the commands of human beings merely. There exists, for the positivist, no necessary connections between law and morals, or between law as it is and law as it ought to be. The positivists' legal system is a closed, logical system without need for referring to social aims, policies, or moral standards. So-called "moral judgments," to the positivists, are "value judgments" merely: and value judgments cannot be established or defended by rational argument. This positivistic understanding of justice and law looms large in American courts today.

All law is derived from the religious understanding—that is, all law in the traditional societies of the West; law in totalist states is another matter entirely. Moses came down from Horeb and did justice upon criminous Israelites: the prophet as lawgiver. Solon reformed the laws of Draco: the religious poet as lawgiver. When law is divorced from the moral sanction of religious convictions, presently the law is corrupted by passion, prejudice, private interest, and misguided sentimentality.

"Justice is certain rectitude of mind, whereby a man does what he ought to do in the circumstances confronting him."

Law Without Justice

If an innocent person is sent to prison or if a killer walks free, we are outraged. The legal system assures us, and we expect and demand, that it will seek to "do justice" in criminal cases

Justice as Fairness

It is commonly felt that the rich flaunt the law while the poor break it.

Constitutional and legal standards protecting free speech are in line with those commonly accepted in democratic societies. The state constitutionally guarantees freedom of expression and access to information. These rights have been developed further by several laws, such as the law on broadcast activity and the law on access to information. These laws were revised by and are of relatively high quality, with satisfactory standards.

Rawls spells out what his conception of "justice as fairness" means the guiding idea is that the principles of justice ... are the principles that free and rational persons concerned to further their own interests would accept in an initial position of equality as defining the fundamental terms of their association. These principles are to regulate all further agreements; they specify the kinds of social cooperation that can be entered into and the forms of government that can be established. (TJ, p. 11)

He locates himself in the contractarian tradition:

- Social Norms are rules indicating how individuals ought to behave in specific situation.
- Obedience is a form of social influence in which one or more individuals behave in specific ways in response to direct orders from someone.
- Compliance is a form of social influence in which one or more persons acquiesce to direct requests from one or more others.

The Circumstances of Justice

Recall Hume: circumstances that make justice possible and necessary:

Objective Circumstances

- Coexist geographically and temporally
- Roughly equal physical and mental powers
- Vulnerable to each other (especially to coalitions)
- Moderate scarcity (too harsh: cooperation breaks down; too abundant: no need for cooperation)

Subjective Circumstances

- Each person has own life-plan
- Each person's knowledge and reasoning is incomplete
- Each person's memory and attention is limited
- Judgement is distorted by anxiety and is biased

Formal Conditions on any Principles

- *Generality*: No proper names or rigged definite descriptions (the veil of ignorance)
- *Universality*: Apply to every moral agent, and every moral agent can accept and follow them
- *Publicity*: Everyone can know they are following the same rules
- *Ordering*: Principles should impose a transitive and complete ordering on people's conflicting claims that are not based on threats or pressure
- *Finality*: The buck stops here

In addition to the limited scope of people's participation in the legislative process, the justice dispensation organs of the state is also suffering from ineptitude and fatigue due to mismanagement. The delay in court proceedings and a failing policing system are two classic examples. For an ordinary Indian, the courts in India make a mockery of the term 'justice' by delaying proceedings for years. Long periods of delays are often exploited by those who can manipulate the system.

Law enforcement agencies are also exploited and manipulated by the same group of individuals. Instead of serving the general public, the law enforcement agencies in India often tend to serve those who have power and money. It appears that the law enforcing agencies in fact allow themselves to be manipulated so that these agencies could also exploit the resulting opportunity for their benefit. The result is selective justice, often to the detriment of the ordinary people. This situation also facilitates widespread corruption in the society.

For the ordinary person the presence of justice is evident in the functioning of the local police and the local courts. These are the two important institutions in any state structure that provide protection and guarantee to a person's life and property. Due to the proximity of these two institutions to the people and their life, the functioning of these institutions is under the constant scrutiny of the people. When these institutions fail to perform reasonably well, the people will exploit its weakness and will also disregard them.

A failing judiciary, inept law enforcement agencies and widespread corruption is the cocktail for disharmony and violence. The convergence of the failing justice mechanisms is the meltdown of the public perception of the justice by the state. When the state fails to provide security and guarantee to its own people, people take law into their own arms. The result is what India is experiencing today.

Such experiences do not suggest that India is poised to become a leading economy by 2020, but is the death knell of an alarmingly weakened and failing democracy.

On one level, it's easy to understand why there is public support for vigilante-style justice: There are more than 20 million cases pending in various Indian courts. Criminal cases drag on for years, with the rich and powerful often getting acquitted. Conviction rates are abysmal:

Incidents of mob justice are becoming common. The growing number of incidents of quick and rough mob justice show that the people no longer have faith in the criminal justice system of the country. People have started believing in vigilantism, taking laws in their own hands and delivering instant justice. This is an ominous trend and augurs ill for law enforcement and order maintenance in the country.

Today, the country is witnessing a surge in crime and lawlessness. In states like Bihar, vast rural areas remain under-policed and at the mercy of lawless elements. In India, in 2004, as many as 60,28,781 cognizable crimes had been reported. When compared to 2003, the crime rate increased by 7.9 per cent. But the fact is that there is massive under-reporting of crime. Even by a very conservative estimate actual incidence of crime should be 10 times more than what it is reported. Non-registration of cases by the police, particularly in the rural areas, is very common. It is a grotesque violation of human rights and forces many people to take law in their own hands and punish criminals.

One very important reason for non-registration, as forcefully highlighted by the National Police Commission in its report, is the anxiety of state governments to keep the crime figures low so as to claim before the state legislature, public and press that crime is well under control. However, even the suppressed crime figures cannot conceal the hard fact that violent crimes are increasing. The difficult and deteriorating crime situation is further compounded by the fact that most criminals go unpunished. Figures of disposal of cases in the courts of law compiled by the National Crimes Record Bureau for 2004 show that 83 per cent of IPC cases are pending trial in various courts.

It is evident that trials conducted by the courts have not kept pace with time. Though the overall conviction rate in respect of criminal cases is 42 per cent, conviction in respect of heinous crimes, as pointed out in the report of Malimath Committee, is just 10 per cent. That is why vigilantism enjoys a considerable degree of ground-level support. It occurs when there is a perceived weakness in the ability of the formal criminal justice system to respond promptly to deal with crime and violence. So long as this gap remains, vigilantes seek to take on responsibilities of the formal criminal justice system. In the event of prolonged and widespread vigilantism (as is the case in Bihar), vigilante groups seek to usurp power reserved for criminal justice system.

Sometimes vigilantism is wrongly equated with self-defence. Vigilante behaviour is premeditative while self-defence is spontaneous. Vigilantes do not care for the police to finish their investigation and courts to punish the offenders. They seek swift and sure punishment. Lynch mobs, as psychologists point out, arm themselves with a sense of retributive righteousness. They mean to exert social control by exemplary doses of terror on the notion that the violence is the only language that the victims understand.

What is sometimes overlooked is that vigilantism can be quite popular among the police officers. Research studies of vigilante groups in New York found that many police officers approved vigilante groups and their methods. There are known instances where police officers join the mob and encourage them to take law in their own hands and mete out instant justice to criminals.

The temptation to take law in one's own hands is much greater when people believe that they can get away playing vigilantes. It is necessary for the police and political authorities to deal firmly with vigilantism, making clear that this form of criminal activity will be put down firmly. Do-it-yourself justice represents a serious threat to democracy and to the rule of law.

Although politicians (and the media) tend to regard mob justice as collective hysteria and moral failure, quite clearly it is intimately connected with public frustration over the nation's collapsing law, order and justice systems. India has a mere 1,000 policemen per million people (*cf.* 3,000 in the US and 2,100 in Australia), and in most of the 485 districts of rural India, the writ of the police doesn't run after 6 p.m. The Indian legal system characterised by archaic procedures and pervasive corruption has accumulated a backlog of over 30 million cases. Little wonder with public confidence in the law, order and justice systems at an all-time low, people are resorting to vigilantism and mob justice.

Curiously the ground reality that India has fewer than 13 judges per million people, whereas the UK has 50, Canada 75 and the US 107, doesn't seem to trouble the consciences of politicians or the public. And even the 13,000 judges countrywide grudgingly employed by government are provided abysmal infrastructure and support services. Government expenditure on the legal system aggregates a mere 0.42 percent of GDP annually *cf.* 4.3 percent in the UK.

Rising vigilantism and recourse to rough and ready mob justice is also fed by the conspicuous failure of state governments to arrest and file charges against vigilante groups. In none of the horrific incidents of mob violence detailed above, have arrests been made by the police. Such inaction and condonation of vigilantism is tantamount to tacit approval of on-the-spot mob justice.

However elimination of lynch justice and establishing the rule of law requires more than mere moral exhortation. Criminal—perhaps deliberate—neglect of law and order and judicial infrastructure are issues which need to be urgently addressed and remedied. If not, dispensation of rough-n-ready mob justice will become the rule rather than exception in shining, fast-track India.

Social Justice

A desire for justice is instinctive in the human character and is a driving force in social progress. Concepts of justice and their application touch on every aspect of human life: perceived injustices lie at the root of much social unrest... While a system of law is a hallmark and measure of civilized society, a truly just society is defined by more than its judicial system, however well considered, conceived and applied it may be. Those laws are needed to safeguard society from recidivist and disruptive elements is, in today's society, all too evident. But however effective they are in protecting society, they are of but limited success in eradicating the causes of anti-social behaviour, and, if inaptly applied, may lead to a perception of justice not being done. Clearly, law alone cannot achieve a just and cohesive society. It also requires, if the daily life of the community is to reflect the noblest qualities of human character, a transformation in the hearts and minds of its members. Such a transformation will not easily be achieved. It will require dedicated and prolonged attention to all aspects of social life, including strengthening the family.

Equity and justice do not require that everyone have access to the same quantity, quality, and variety of food, clothing or shelter, or that food, clothing, and shelter be equally convenient or effortless for all. Equity and justice are matters of ensuring equal access to *specific* things to which all have equal rights—not equal access to *all* things. A right to safe, nutritious food, for example, does not imply a right to prime rib and artichoke hearts nor to packaged or pre-prepared foods.

A Pillar of Government

Justice, described four hundred years ago as one of the four pillars of government, has long concerned philosophers, theologians and jurists. More than one ancient insight finds echoes in modern theory, although Plato's remarkable perception that justice was a condition of the human heart or soul to be cultivated through education has not received the attention it deserved. While rejecting earlier ideas of justice as an imposition to benefit those in authority, the administration of justice in Plato's 'ideal society' nevertheless still divided its citizenry into classes, together ruled by 'philosopher-kings' who would regulate all social activity and determine each person's place within that society—a society within which 'the better class controls the inferior'. Approaches such as this can still be found today: the distinguishing between citizen and non-citizen, between male and female; between the faithful and unbelievers; between the property-owning and the indigent; or between races and cultures. In modern thinking, Michael Walzer assumes that separate communities will each arrive at their own understanding of justice and the 'good society'; while John Rawls emphasised the rights of the individual over the greater good of a society that was assumed to be essentially Western and democratic in nature.

Why Social Justice is Important

While the idea of social justice begins with Aristotle, the Philosopher's contribution was more in the nature of an error than a discovery. According to Aristotle and numbers of commentators down to the present day, the common good was a nebulous concept having more to do with the general welfare and collective well-being than anything specific. Being nebulous, it was, as one might expect, not directly accessible by the action or actions of any one individual. That is, regardless of intent, there was nothing definite in the common good on which to act directly, therefore, no direct act on the common good was possible—by definition.

This resulted in the situation where the individual was regarded as virtually helpless in social situations when it came to making any changes or improvements for the better. Only the individual with the greatest degree and broadest scope of virtue could hope to affect the common good and that only indirectly. That meant the "philosopher king" was a necessity, for he was defined as being the individual with the greatest virtue in the state.

Still, the philosopher king was as profoundly helpless as any other individual when addressing the problem of restructuring the common good. The common good was not considered a definite thing, and, therefore, nothing definite could be done to it or with it. The philosopher king or any other ruler was restricted to passing laws and hoping that things came out at least marginally the way intended.

The individual was not regarded as being able to access the common good directly. This meant that he was fundamentally alienated from society itself. This in turn meant that every human being was not naturally a member of society, in spite of Aristotle's recognition of the fact that man was social by nature. This explained the problem of individual helplessness in the face of social problems, and reinforced the idea of mere existence as a condition of constant warfare.

What is Social Justice?

All of the difficulty with attempting to affect the common good indirectly changed with Pius XI's development of a completed theory of social virtue. Pius XI started by accepting the fact and all the implications of man being social by nature. He followed this with the idea that society was intrinsically social. Society was not just a collection of individuals, but of individuals coming together and associating in groups. Groups are specifically social creations. This means that the common good, while broadly, if precisely, defined as the capacity to acquire and develop all virtue (that which all men have in common), also takes on concrete form as the aggregation of groups—institutions. These embody the ways, means, and formal "social transactions" developed within a society to assist the individual members of society in their task of acquiring and developing virtue. The common good becomes directly accessible by every human being, not just philosopher kings.

Pius XI introduced the idea of a class of virtue that was not directed at the good of the individual, but at the good of society as a whole. Social virtue is directed at the good of the common good, or, perhaps, more clearly, toward the health of those institutions of the common good which are designed to assist us in our task of acquiring and developing individual virtue. To repeat, this new class of virtue, let us call it "social virtue" (for that's what it is), is not directed toward assisting any individual in his acquisition and development of individual good or goods. Social virtue is, on the contrary, directed toward assisting the institutions of society in maintaining or reforming themselves so as to enable them to assist individuals in acquiring and developing individual good or goods.

To put it yet another way, social virtue is not directed at assisting individual members of society to acquire and develop virtue, but at helping institutions acquire and develop the structures that assist individual members of society in acquiring and developing virtue. Social virtue is, therefore, by definition, directed toward the *common* good, not the *individual* good of any member or members of society, regardless how numerous they might be.

That is a difficult concept to understand. People have been misunderstanding it since Pius XI first began teaching it. The result has been that, just as they have for thousands of years, people still attempt to reform the social order through the application, more or less intensive, of the individual virtues.

What is this Mess We're in?

The individual virtues, while absolutely necessary for the individual and his spiritual and social health, are simply not adequate to the task of maintaining the social health of institutions. This is because individual virtues are specifically individual. Virtues that are specifically individual are not the proper "tool" for addressing problems that are specifically social.

There is a great deal of confusion over the meaning of social justice, some of which may have been intentionally caused. Nowhere is this more evident than when we consider the confusion over the difference between distributive justice (an individual virtue) and social justice (a social virtue).

Sometimes erroneously construed as "social justice,"3 the classic notion of distributive justice, like commutative justice, is based on equality, but an equality of proportion. Aristotle defined distributive justice as a proportionality of value given and received rather than a strict equality or equivalence of value. Where commutative justice is concerned with the relationship of "other to other," distributive justice deals with the relationship of the "social whole" to the "social parts." Distributive justice is, therefore, but only in that limited sense *a* "social justice." Distributive justice is not *the* social justice, for it has as its object the individual good of each of the members of a group. Social justice has as its special object the common good of all mankind. Equating the particular virtue of social justice with distributive justice is a logical "fallacy of equivocation," for the word "social" is used differently in describing the two types of justice

Demonstrating the extent to which "consultors" have managed to distort traditional understandings of principles and concepts, the *Catechism* defines distributive justice as that justice "which regulates what the community owes its citizens in proportion to their contributions *and needs*."6 [Emphasis added.] The "and needs" add-on is directly contrary to the definition given in the *Summa*, which describes distributive justice as that virtue "whereby a ruler or a steward gives to each what his rank *deserves*."7 [Emphasis added.] The popular commentary on the Summa by Msgr. Paul J. Glenn, *A Tour of the Summa*, 8 restates this passage in the following manner. "There is another type of justice, called distributive, which consists in the bestowal of good according to the *needs* of the receiver." [Emphasis added.] There is a significant difference, however, in what an individual *deserves* and what he *needs*. I may need many things, but I cannot justly receive them until I have offered something in equal or proportionate exchange.

To understand Aquinas, other than simply reading what he actually wrote as opposed to what commentators choose to revise or restate, we have to realize that, in a very real sense, the *Summa* is itself a commentary on Aristotle. Unless the Angelic Doctor makes it very explicit and offers substantially more commentary than a mere restatement of the Philosopher's definition, we must assume that Aquinas means exactly what Aristotle meant. When interpreting Aquinas, the thought of Aristotle, except when otherwise indicated, should be taken as normative. There is no such indication in this case.

There is also the problem that many people confuse the special meanings of words used by Aquinas. "Ruler," "steward," "gives" and "deserves" all create problems if the casual reader or commentator with an agenda fail to link the passage above from the description of God's Nature with the fuller description and explanations in the discussion on "Justice" in the Second Part.

Most immediately dangerous for our purposes is the confusion of the words used to describe "group" or "institution." There is an automatic equation on the part of many commentators of "community" in Aquinas and Aristotle with "state." They presume not only that distributive justice covers all distributions from any kind of authority (not true, as Aquinas points out), but that the state is somehow the only legitimate form of civil or temporal authority. This idea is inevitably combined with the idea that the Aristotelian act of legal justice and the Thomist act of social justice are one and the same. The only possible outcome is an intense worship of the state as the sole agent for regulating and maintaining the common good not just of civil society, but of all the societies of man, civil, religious and domestic.

The state does confer its benefits according to distributive justice. All distributions, however, are not, *ipso facto*, distributive justice. In the instance of a distribution based on need, the state is standing in for the failure of charity or *commutative* justice by individual citizens or for the sake of expedience and efficiency. This is allowed under the principle of double effect.

Distribution on the basis of need comes under a special form of commutative justice, since extreme need is considered to render what is ordinarily private property common property. This means that the individual in dire need has the right to exercise property in what ordinarily belongs to another. Since it is concerned with property and the exercise of a right, this comes under "proprietary justice." Proprietary justice is a commutative justice, not a distributive justice.

When making a distribution based on need, the state is not functioning as the proper efficient cause of justice, but as an agent for the efficient cause—the individual on whom an individual in dire need is dependent. Simply inserting the state into the transaction does not, *ipso facto*, render it distributive justice. In addition, distributive justice can only be construed to cover a distribution based on need if "poverty" is understood as conferring a "status" that contributes to the community. On the contrary, poverty renders an individual the proper object of charity, not of justice.

How did we get here?

At the risk of sounding unpastoral, I believe the blame for this state of affairs can be placed squarely on the shoulders of the bishops. The earlier encyclicals were largely addressed to the pope's brother bishops. It was and remains their responsibility to study, understand, and internalize the teachings in the documents in order to disseminate them to the faithful. The fault of the bishops as a whole is seen both in those who misinterpreted the documents and in those who did no interpretation or teaching at all, letting things drop or their staffs take over their teaching function.

The popes obviously know what has been happening. The later encyclicals, particularly those of John Paul II, are increasingly addressed not exclusively to the bishops in their role as chief teachers in their dioceses, but to all the faithful, and even, on occasion, to everyone of good will. This demonstrates that the popes, unable to delegate effectively to those unwilling or unable to assume the burdens of teaching, have been forced to take over the role of direct teacher of the whole Church.

As John Paul II has pointed out, we are faced with a plague of relativism. There is immense confusion between what constitutes principle and the application of principle. There is a lack of adequate response to various trends in modern society, selling out to the secular in most cases instead of resisting it or converting it. When there is a response, it is usually individualistic and therefore, by definition, inadequate to the task of overcoming a social problem.

There are many reasons for this confusion aside from the main one of widespread misunderstanding of the work of Pius XI in the social virtues, especially social justice. Primarily, it is because there has been a general severance of religion from daily life, as well as a consequent failure to have or use a consistent philosophy other than relativism or secularism in approaching the problems of daily life and applying specific principles to their solution. This prevalence of relativism has infected the interpretation of the social encyclicals. The growth of relativism and expedience as the basic approach to social problems is matched only by the growth of its inevitable handmaiden in the social order—the rise of fascism in all its forms.

This is understandable, for the oxymoronic "social justice without Pius XI" leads inevitably to fascism through its dependence on the state as the prime agent of all social change and maintenance of the common good. As a result, Pius XI's understanding of social virtue in general and social justice in particular has been excluded, either by design or lack of understanding, from the development of social thought and the design and maintenance of our social institutions for almost a century. Without Pius XI, we end up only in fascism. With Pius XI, we can attain the Reign of Christ the King. The condition of society throughout the world makes it apparent that we are rapidly approaching the point where any possible middle ground is disappearing.

One significant aspect of this whole problem is that various elements, for whatever reason, both misunderstood or twisted the teachings of Pius XI and seized on the vagueness that came after him to promote various agendas. This was based on a failure to understand and internalize the principles of social restructuring—which was in turn due to the failure of Catholic Action. What we ended up with is a "cafeteria-style" method of interpretation that led to a necessary vagueness. The accepted way to interpret the social teachings of the Church these days is to take them anyway you want, project your private interpretation back on Pius XI and Leo XIII, and dismiss the inevitable contradictions as "stray rhetorical fragments" or "prudential matter."

Why did we get here?

The effort to undermine the true sense of the social teachings of the Church has a specific orientation. There has been a hijacking of the whole concept of social justice to meet various political agendas. Ultimately, these consist, at heart, at aiming at nothing less than control of the Church. The struggles detailed by Msgr. George Kelly in, among other works, *The Battle for the American Church*11 and Dr. Ralph McInerny in *What Went Wrong With Vatican II*12 reveal an unremitting effort directed at control of the Church. The goal is to make the Church not only in the world, but of it. This must be done, and done completely in order that the temporal order can force whatever current vision it has of reality on to the Church. Thus the Church will change from a censuring guide and go along with, or, more likely, offer enthusiastic approbation of every change in temporal society, no matter how greatly it may be at odds with reality, that is, with God's Nature.

The only quarrel I would have with either of these two commentators is that Dr. McInerny asserted as his premise that the Second Vatican Council was not the beginning of the institutionalization of dissent. On the contrary, according to Dr. McInerny, this move came somewhat later, with the promulgation of *Humanæ Vitæ*. I disagree. The Second Vatican Council was not the beginning of the institutionalization of dissent—we do agree there—but I consider its genesis as coming much earlier. The surge of dissent reached its height with the rapid growth of Modernism early in the twentieth century. This was ably halted, but not effectively reduced or countered, by Saint Pope Pius X. The cancer remained, although in remission, until the opportunity offered by the social upheaval coeval with the promulgation of *Humanæ Vitæ*.

The infection of Modernism joined in a synergistic alliance the lack of explicit support and iteration of both the specific thought and the precise language of Pius XI by subsequent popes. Added to this was the failure of the bishops throughout the world to carry out their teaching function effectively and properly. In support of this contention, I need only cite the change that slipped into the definition of "distributive justice," described above. This was outside of papal documents, true, but still embodied many people's understanding of the encyclicals.

The complete change in meaning from the classical understanding of distributive justice may have derived from Msgr. John Ryan, who, unknowingly, may have been infected with the attitudes of Modernism, though not the explicit doctrines of the movement. That attitude is the virtual mandate found in Modernism and other relativistic philosophies to interpret every dictum of the Church from a personal "situational" perspective based on the desire of the moment rather than eternal truth. This results in twisting the teachings of the Church in order to get what you want, regardless of the consequences.

THE SOCIAL VISION OF PIUS XI

What was Pius XI talking about? His goal was nothing less than the complete reformation and restructuring of the social order so as to institute and maintain the Reign of Christ the King. That requires some explanation. The correct understanding of the Reign of Christ the King supersedes the somewhat simplistic ideas that have been forced onto the general understanding of the concept.

The Reign of Christ the King is the establishment of a specific state of society. Society is run in accordance with universal moral principles, as interpreted and defined—but not enforced—by the Church through the Magisterium, the bishops in communion with the pope, and the pope in his office as universal and infallible teacher in matters of faith and morals.

The Reign of Christ the King is primarily civil, but includes domestic and religious society insofar as they impinge on the civil order. Attaining and maintaining the Reign of Christ the King is the goal and aim of Catholic Action, the organization and movement adapted by Pius XI to carry out his vision.

We need to realize that an interpreter and guide is not a ruler. A "Christian society" in the sense meant by "The Reign of Christ the King" does not mean control of the civil order or direct rule by the Church. Nor does it mean that everyone or even a determinant number of the people must be Catholic or even Christian, however else that might be desirable for their personal salvation.

No, having the Church as guide for civil society and interpreter of the universal moral values that must underpin the social order means that there must be a single authoritative source for such interpretation and guidance. The Church, by divine ordinance, was prepared and instituted for that role in the world. This role of the Church does not mean that interpretation of natural law from a source other than the Church must therefore, *ipso fact*o, be wrong or in error, as the recent document from the Congregation for the Doctrine of the Faith made clear. No one has a monopoly on the truth. As Pius XI pointed out, in the Church is found the fullness of truth in totality, not exclusively.

She has never maintained that outside her fold and apart from her teaching, man cannot arrive at any moral truth; she has on the contrary more than once condemned this opinion because it has appeared under more forms than one. She does however say, has said, and will ever say, that because of her institution by Jesus Christ, because of the Holy Ghost sent her in His name by the Father, she alone possesses what she has had immediately from God and can never lose, the whole of moral truth, *omnem veritatem*, in which all individual moral truths are included, as well those which man may learn by the help of reason, as those which form part of revelation or which may be deduced from it.

Conceivably, although I think it highly unlikely, it would be possible in this sense to have a "Christian" society without any Christians. This would be possible only in the sense that a society was founded on universal moral principles as interpreted by the Church. Society would be guided in such a way that the application of the principles in no wise departed from the application that would have been recommended had the direct guidance of the Church been known or sought.

Etymology

The word "lynching" is recorded in English since 1835, as a verb derived from the earlier expression *Lynch law* (known since 1811). This phrase is likely named after the Lynch family whose surname derives either from Old English *hlinc* "hill" or from Irish *Loingseach* "sailor".

The most likely eponym for the concept of Lynch law as summary justice is William Lynch, the author of "Lynch's Law", an agreement with the Virginia General Assembly (Virginian state legislature) on September 22, 1782, which allowed Lynch to pursue and punish criminals in Pittsylvania County, without due process of law, because legal proceedings were in practical terms impossible in the area due to the lack of adequate provision of courts. The Webster's Dictionary of 1913 poses a counterargument that "Lynch law is said to be derived from a Virginian named Lynch, who took the law into his own hands. But the origin of the term is very doubtful."

Others believe the term came into use only with Colonel Charles Lynch, a Virginia magistrate and officer on the revolutionary side during the American Revolutionary War, who in any case continued William's practice, as the head of a vigilance committee, an irregular court, trying and sentencing to fining and imprisoning petty criminals and pro-British "Tories" in his district circa 1782.

In these cases only minor punishments were used, mostly corporal punishment, especially flogging. Neither William Lynch nor Charles Lynch ever executed anyone.

Extralegal punishments similar to those adopted by both Lynches continued to be duplicated by others in the newly independent U.S.A. and elsewhere. The term "lynch law" came in to general use as a loosely employed description of efforts to maintain the established order either by the use of actual lynchings against those who would change it, or even their mere threat, which often proved sufficient to silence activists and critics. The term *Lynch mob*—for a group of private persons who collectively practice lynching—is attested from 1838. Since the Reconstruction Period following the American Civil War, it came to mean, generally, the summary infliction of capital punishment. The further narrowing of the meaning to extralegal execution specifically by hanging, is from the 20th century.

Alternative Theories

Another suggestion is that it came from Lynchs Creek, South Carolina, where summary justice was also administered to outlaws; some writers even attempted to trace it to Ireland, or to England.

One popular and widespread theory, repeated for example by Joseph Edwin Proffit in the introduction to *Lynching: Its Cause and Cure* Yale Law Journal, Vol. 7, No. 6 (Mar., 1898), pp. 264-267, and frequently elsewhere, traces the term to an event in 1493 when James FitzStephen Lynch, mayor and warden of Galway (Ireland), tried and executed his own son. Lynch was a member of one of the most powerful of the fourteen Tribes of Galway, the families of Anglo-Norman magnates who dominated the city and region during the period. The legend, recited in more detail in Hardiman's 1820 History of Galway had it that Lynch's son, Walter murdered a Spaniard named Gomez in a brawl over a young woman named Agnes; Lynch was then faced with a situation where no Galwegian would risk the enmity of the Lynch clan by participating in a trial or execution of the son. Worse still, Gomez had been an invited guest of the Lynch family, effectively under their protection, and under the customs of the time his unpunished murder was a grave stain on the family honour. Consequently Lynch felt obliged to carry out the trial and execution himself. If true, the legend is also factually inconsistent with the practice of lynching, in that the son was validly guilty and Lynch himself a magistrate with the authority to try someone for such a crime, *i.e.*, the trial was not as such extrajudicial, rather it was the relation of the judge and executioner to the executed that was notable. Moreover, if Hardiman is to be believed, the mob favored the release of the unfortunate Walter Lynch, in marked contrast to the usual situation at a lynching. Suggestions that the son was hung from the window of Lynch's own home are probably apocryphal, driven by the fact that the alleged window still exists, set in the stone facade of the 14th century Lynch townhouse (known as Lynch's Castle) in Market Street at the side of St. Nicholas' Church, with an inset stone plaque of a skull, dated 1624, commemorating the event (apparently then a source of some pride to the Lynch 'tribe.') The theory would also leave a transatlantic, centuries-wide gap between the event and the earliest records of the use of "Lynch law" or "lynching." However, the most significant detail undermining the theory that this 1493 event is the origin of the phrase, is Hardiman's failure to remark on the use of the words "Lynch Law" or "lynching" in his extensive 1820 treatment of the tale, indicating that the terms' common use arose *post*-1820.

A popular theory around Asia is that it is derived from a historical death penalty pronounced as "lingchi" # or slow slicing in China and Korea.

United States

Lynch Law, a form of mob violence and putative justice, usually involving (but by no means restricted to) the illegal hanging of suspected criminals, was common in the Southern United States from the mid-19th to the mid-20th centuries. Before the Civil War, its victims were usually black slaves and persons suspected of aiding escaped slaves; lynching was mainly a frontier phenomenon. However, during Reconstruction, the Ku Klux Klan and others used lynching as a means to curb what they viewed as excesses within the Radical Republican Reconstruction government. Federal troops operating under the Civil Rights Act of 1871 largely broke up the Reconstruction-era Klan, but with the end of Reconstruction in 1877, white southerners regained nearly exclusive control of the region's governments and courts. Lynchings declined, but were by no means brought to an end. In 1892, 161 African-Americans were lynched. The largest single lynching incident in America's history was the lynching of 11 Italian-Americans in New Orleans, Louisiana in 1892. This incident was popularized in the HBO movie "Vendetta".

Lynching in the United States was usually a racial victimization. Most lynchings were committed by the KKK.

After the 1915 release of the movie *The Birth of a Nation,* which glorified the Reconstruction-era Klan, the Klan re-formed and re-adopted lynching as a means to socially, economically, and politically terrorize and paralyze black populations. Victims were usually black men, often accused of assaulting or raping whites. Lynch Law declined sharply after 1935, and there have been no reported incidents of this type since the late 1960s.

This memorial to the 1920 Duluth lynchings was described by its artist as attempting to "reinvest [the victims] with their unique personalities", to counteract the way the lynchings "depersonalized" them.

The executions of 4,743 people who were lynched in the United States between 1882 and 1968 were not often publicized. It is likely that many more unrecorded lynchings occurred in this period. Lynching statistics were kept only for the 86 years between 1882 and 1968, and were based primarily on newspaper accounts. Yet the socio-political impact of lynchings could be significant, as illustrated by the restoration in 1901 of capital punishment in the state of Colorado (which had abolished it only in 1897) as the result of a lynching outbreak in 1900.

Most lynchings were inspired by unsolved crime, racism, and innuendo. 3,500 of its victims were African Americans. Lynchings took place in every state except four, but were concentrated in the Cotton Belt (Mississippi, Georgia, Alabama, Texas and Louisiana).

Members of mobs that participated in these public murders often took photographs of what they had done, and those photographs, distributed on postcards, were collected by James Allen who has now published them online, and written words to accompany the images.

In 2007 the Jena Six incident in Jena, Louisiana demonstrated the ongoing cultural significance of lynching, as nooses tied to a tree recalled the history of lynchings.

Europe

In Europe early examples of a similar phenomenon are found in the proceedings of the *Vehmgerichte* in medieval Germany, and of Lydford law, gibbet law or Halifax law, Cowper justice and Jeddart justice in the thinly settled and border districts of Great Britain.

In 1944, Wolfgang Rosterg, a German POW known to be unsympathetic to the Nazi regime in Germany, was lynched by Nazi fanatics in prisoner of war Camp 21 in Comrie, Scotland. After the end of the war, five of the perpetrators were hanged at Pentonville Prison—the largest multiple execution in 20th century Britain.

There are also some personal accounts of lynching in Budapest, Hungary, during the 1956 Hungarian Revolution against the occupying Soviets.

Mexico

On November 23 2004, in the Tlahuac lynching, three Mexican undercover federal agents doing a narcotics investigation were lynched in the town of San Juan Ixtayopan (Mexico City) by an angry crowd who saw them taking photographs and mistakenly suspected they were trying to abduct children from a primary school. The policemen identified themselves immediately but were held and beaten for several hours before two of them were killed and set on fire. The whole incident was covered by the media almost from the beginning, including their pleas for help and their murder. By the time police rescue units arrived, two of the policemen were reduced to charred corpses and the third was seriously injured. Authorities suspect the lynching was provoked by the persons being investigated.

Both local and federal authorities abandoned them to their fate, saying the town was too far away to even try to arrive in time and some officials stating they would provoke a massacre if they tried to rescue them from the mob.

Dominican Republic

Anti-black and anti-Haitian bias has long been a part of Dominican identity and culture. According to an Amnesty International report, lynching of Haitians and black Dominicans have continued to occur as late as 2006.

South Africa

The practice of whipping and necklacing offenders and political opponents evolved in the 1980s during the apartheid era in South Africa. Residents of black townships lost confidence in the apartheid judicial system and formed "people's courts" that authorized whip lashings and deaths by necklacing. Necklacing is a term used to describe the torture and execution of victims by igniting a rubber, kerosene-filled, tire that has been forced around the victim's chest and arms. Necklacing was used to punish numerous victims, including children, who were alleged to be traitors to the black liberation movement as well as relatives and associates of the offenders. The practice was endorsed by Winnie Mandela, wife of the imprisoned Nelson Mandela and a senior member of the African National Congress.

PRESSURE FOR LAW

Starting in the 1890s, African Americans in the North and South, and their white allies, built an anti-lynching movement which used diverse strategies to confront these outrages. They used not only petitions, letter-writing, marches, and rallies, but also plays, songs, visual art, films, and cartoons to assert the humanity of the victims, educate the public about the scope of the problem, and pressure politicians to pass a federal anti-lynching law. While this movement ebbed and flowed and never did achieve its legislative goal, it became an important current within the "river," as historian Vincent Harding has called it of the freedom struggle.

The anti-lynching movement confronted not only the violent acts that became known as "lynching," but also images of those acts which sought to lionize the mob and dehumanize their victims. Often, an enterprising photographer or, as time went on and technology allowed, an amateur in possession of a Kodak or a Brownie camera

That is the whole idea of social justice and the role it is to fill in reforming and restructuring the social order. The problem with much of what passes for "social justice" these days is clearly at variance with the intentions, both expressed and implied, of Pius XI when he made his fundamental and profound breakthrough in moral philosophy. Grasping the real idea of what Pius XI meant takes some work, however. Perhaps we should not be too surprised that man's inherent laziness, an inevitable consequence of his fallen state, kicks in and we go with what seems most comfortable for us, relatively speaking. What we end up with is social justice without Pius XI.

Equality

Equality according to justice and equality according to friendship are different. In justice equality is primarily according to merit, but in friendship it is primarily according to quantity<that is, the more unequal two people with regard to wealth, virtue, status, etc., the more unlikely it will be for a friendship to develop. Because most people wish to be liked more than to like, most people like flatterers, who are friends in an inferior position. Being liked by someone is akin to being honored by him. People like to be honored by good men in order to assure their own good opinion of themselves. However, people enjoy being liked not for the sake of something else but for its own sake. Friendship also seems to be chosen for its own sake, but it seems to depend more on liking than on being liked, as in the case of a mother's love for a child in spite of the child's response.

Both friendship and justice seem to be concerned with the same things and the same people, and every association involves a mix of justice and friendship. The degree of injustice of a harm done to another depends on the degree of friendship that exists between the two people. Political associations are formed for the sake of the expedient, and all other associations are a subdivision of this. The kinds of friendship that exists among those in the association corresponds to the type of association.

Forms of Government

There are three forms of government and their corresponding deviations. The three good forms of government in order from best to least good are

- kingship,
- aristocracy and
- timocracy (or democracy),

and the three deviations are,

- respectively,
- tyranny, oligarchy
- and mob rule.

Of the three deviations, tyranny is the worst, and mob rule is the least evil. Kingship is somewhat like a father's rule of a family. Tyranny is like the rule of master over his slaves. In aristocracy people rule based on merit, in timocracy they rule based on honor, and in oligarchy they rule based on wealth.

Friendship in each form of government exists to the extent that justice exists. A king is a friend to his subjects because he wishes to make them good. In aristocracy the friendship is by virtue of a relationship of superiority based on merit, and in timocracy there is friendship based on equality. There is little friendship in the deviant forms of government. Of the three corrupt forms of government, friendship is mostly likely to arise under mob rule.

Chapter 7

Social Control

"The greater the number of laws and enactments, the more thieves and robbers there will be."

—*Lao-tzu, Chinese philosopher (c. 604-531 B.C.)*

Questionable actions need to be defended when we are considered to be responsible for an undesirable or odd outcome. Offering such a defense should then refer to (a) our responsibility, and (b) the undesirable or odd nature of the outcome. When we are held responsible for an undesirable situation, we are to explain the reasons for our actions in order that it will bring about an evaluation of the situation or the outcome whereby it no longer will seem so negative.

Two types of explanation may be discerned:

(a) Justification, and
(b) Excuse.

- *Justification:* An explanation which is aimed at eliminating or lessening the negative value of the outcome of a questionable action.
- *Excuse:* An explanation which is aimed at eliminating or lessening our responsibility for a questionable action.

Excuses and Emotions

The relationship between excuses and emotions can be summarized by a few central points:

1. Questionable actions, specifically when they involve damage, may cause negative emotions in those being hurt, and in some cases, also in those that caused the damage.
2. Excuses are explanations aimed to repair one's self image, the emotional damage related with the loss of that self-image and the emotional damage caused to another agent, while trying to protect the listener from being emotionally hurt (cf. Weiner *et al.*, 1991). Excuses typically do little by way of repairing the emotional damage caused, but usually succeed well where restoring one's self image is concerned and the emotional uneasiness associated with it.
3. An excuse may, under some circumstances, cause further aggravation of the emotional tension between the parties involved, or even be the factor that will cause such a tension to arise, because of two main factors: (a) as an usually unsatisfactory explanation, it may be perceived as continuing or even initiating the same sort of undesirable behaviour evolved by the questionable action, namely, hurting the listener; (b) when it fails to be accepted by the other side, the excuse maker may view this as a violation of the relationship and trust, especially when from his/her point of view the excuse given contains a satisfactory explanation.

Social Control consists of the forces and processes that encourage conformity. Three factors combine to create social control.

1. Internalization is the process of building norms and values from our groups into our self concept.
2. Informal social control is self restraint exercised because of a fear of what others may think.
3. Formal social controls are administrative sanctions such as fines and imprisonment.

Formal Social Controls

A. The role of the police is to investigate and arrest persons suspected of committing crimes.
   1. The police are in a unique and powerful position due to their ability to make arrests under conditions of low visibility and great discretion.
   2. The discretionary powers are best reflected in street-level *justice* or the decisions made by police in the initial stages of an investigation.

B. The court system involves the prosecution of people who have been arrested as suspects in the commission of a crime.
   1. Decision stages in the court system are critical in that negotiation and plea bargaining account for 90 per cent of all convictions. They occur before a trial can be held.
   2. Sentencing varies greatly from jurisdiction to jurisdiction with prejudice and class bias playing a strong role.

C. The prison system is assigned the task of administering punishment to those convicted of crimes. Five rationalizations for punishment are *retribution*, *reformation*, *specific deterrence*, *general deterrence* and *prevention*.

A society must have *social order* if it is to function smoothly. A society maintains *social control* over its members in three principal ways. First, it socializes them so that they will want to behave as they should. Second, society imposes *group pressure* upon the individual so that he must conform or be punished by his group. This group pressure may be expressed through the informal controls of the primary group—approval and disapproval, praises, scorn, ostracism, etc.; or it may operate through the more formal controls of secondary groups—rules and regulations, standardized procedures, propaganda, rewards, titles, and penalties. Finally, control through *force* is used where other controls fail. But in many social situations, behaviour is more greatly controlled by the needs and pressures of the situation—the *situational determinants of behaviour*—than by the character one brings to the situation.

Social deviation arises whenever a person fails to conform to the usual norms of the society. Deviation may be individual, in that a person deviates from the normal behaviour of his group; or it may be group deviation, in which the entire group deviates from social norms, so that the individual is a conforming member of a deviant group or subculture. In practice these two types tend to merge, since deviants tend to seek out other deviants and form deviant groups. Deviant's arc also divided into *cultural deviants* and *psychological deviants.* Cultural deviants simply deviate from the expected behaviour norms. Psychological deviants are deviant from the norm in their personality integration; in. their social behaviour they may be either deviant or conformist.

Some forms of deviation are approved—the leader, hero, genius, and saint are often (although not always) honored and revered. Efforts to determine which factors account for outstanding individual achievement are not very conclusive, but it appears that personality factors and social circumstances play a larger role in "greatness" than is generally known.

Many forms of deviation are disapproved by the culture. Deviation through *inability* to conform—often caused by physical or mental defect or illness—is usually viewed with sympathy. The role of social and cultural influences in producing mental illness cannot be exactly measured, but there is widespread agreement that our culture provokes mental conflicts which contribute to mental illness.

Other deviation arises through *failure* to conform, and the causes are debatable. Physical-type theories are popular but unproved. Psychoanalytic theories are popular and plausible, but also unproved. Most of the disapproved individual deviation probably stems, at least partly if not entirely, from failures in socialization, so that the norms and values of the culture are imperfectly integrated into the personality of the individual. The family plays the key role in socialization, and is the main channel through which the child absorbs the culture's norms and values. Unsatisfactory family life is, therefore, the principal factor in disapproved individual deviation. The family, however, is a part of the culture, and unsatisfactory family life is often a reflection of conflicts within the culture. Such conflicts surround cultural norms with uncertainty, and by thus imposing pressures upon individuals, help to produce a state of normlessness called *anomie.* The disharmony between our cultural goals and our means for attaining them encourage anomie and deviation.

Deviation is relative, not absolute, in that most people are deviant to some degree. Wherever a particular pattern of deviation becomes widely followed and excused, it is called a *norm of evasion.* Whenever a culture becomes unbearably confining, norms of evasion are likely to appear. In time these may become the new norms. Thus deviation, while an enemy of social stability, is also a means of introducing the changed norms which become necessary if a changing society is to remain reasonably integrated and efficient.

I. *Crowds and Mobs: Non-routine Collective Action*

   A. *Collective actions* are episodic crowd actions that are prompted by non-routine events. *Social movements* are deliberate, organized attempts to change social institutions from the outside.

B. A crowd is a relatively large number of people drawn to a common location by some non-routine event. Some of the more common types of crowds are: riots, looting, mobs, demonstrations, panics and spectator crowds.

C. Theories of crowd behaviour include contagion theory, convergence theory and the emergent norm theory,

1. *Contagion theory* stresses crowd situations that lead to the development of unanimous and intense feelings and behaviours that are at odds with the usual predispositions of the individual participants. It explains only one type of crowd behaviour: the escalating response.

2. *Convergence theory* contends that the cause or triggering event, for crowd action selectively draws people who share a common set of predispositions.

(a) The convergence of many like-minded people provides the critical mass for their predispositions to be put into action.

(b) The major criticism against convergence theory is that it ignores the heterogeneity of most crowds.

3. *Emergent-norm* theory suggests that each crowd is governed by norms developed and validated by group processes within the crowd. That is, the crowd develops a shared conviction that their behaviour is appropriate to the situation.

II. *Rumor and the Mass Media*

A. A rumor is unauthenticated information spread by word of mouth, they thrive in ambiguous situations where it is impossible to get accurate information. The rumor process involves sharpening, leveling and assimilation.

B. The mass media provide a rapid process that can be vital in creating and sustaining collective behaviour. A *public* is a dispersed group of people interested in and divided over an issue.

CROWDS

An important concept in the study of collective behaviour is the crowd, *a temporary gathering of people who share a common focus of attention and whose members influence one another.* Historian Peter Laslett (1984) claims that in medieval Europe a crowd of 2 5,000 would have formed only when major armies marched into combat. Crowds of this size are routine in large, industrial societies, and are found at football stadiums and even registration halls of large universities.

Herbert Blumer (1969) has identified four types of crowds, partly on the basis of level of emotional intensity.

A *casual crowd* is a loose collection of people who interact little, if at all. People gathered on the heach or observing an automobile accident from a street corner have only a passing awareness of one another. Few social patterns are typical of casual crowds beyond the momentary sharing of an interest.

A *conventional crowd* is the result of deliberate planning of an event, such as an auction, a lecture, or a funeral. Any interaction is likely to conform to conventional norms appropriate to the situation. For example, people hid against one another at an auction according to established rules.

An *expressive crowd* forms around an event that has emotional appeal, such as a religious revival, a wrestling match, or the New Year's Eve celebration in New York's Times Square. People join expressive crowds to share in the excitement caused by the event. This focus on emotional release makes expressive crowds relatively spontaneous. The emotional energy they generate is often exhilarating.

An *acting crowd* is energetically doing something, possibly rushing into a concert hall as the doors are opened or fleeing from a building that is on fire. Acting crowds are often united by emotions even more powerful than those typical of expressive crowds, sometimes reaching feverish intensity that provokes participants to mob violence. In 1985, for example, 60,000 soccer fans assembled in a stadium near Brussels, Belgium, to watch the European Cup Finals between Italy and Great Britain. About forty-five minutes before the start of the game, British fans, many of them reportedly intoxicated, began to taunt Italians sitting beyond a fence in the adjacent section. Next the two sides threw bottles and rocks at each other, until suddenly the British surged toward the Italians, tearing down the fence in a human wave. As an estimated 400 million television viewers watched in horror, a rampaging mob trampled hundreds of helpless spectators. Within minutes, thirty-eight people were dead and another four hundred injured (Lacayo, 1985).

This example illustrates how a crowd can change from one type to another as emotions rise. Sports spectators are typically a conventional crowd, whose activity is limited to cheering and booing and who interact little with one another. In this situation, however, a conventional crowd became an expressive crowd and, provoked by a dramatic event such as name calling, was transformed into an acting crowd on a rampage.

Deliberate action by a crowd is not the product of only rising emotions. Participants in *protest crowds*—a fifth category that can be added to Blumer's list—engage in a variety of actions, such as strikes, boycotts, sit-ins, and protest marches, that have some political goal (McPhail & Wohlstein, 1983). For example, in the middle of a bitter strike in 1986, Hoiniel meat-packing workers from more than a dozen states marched through the streets of Austin, Minnesota, to protest what they contended were unfair practices by the company. Facing financial problems, Hormel had attempted to cut wages and benefits, and the workers decided to challenge this policy publicly.

Protest crowds vary in their emotional energy, sometimes resembling conventional crowds and other times, acting crowds. For example, many public demonstrations during the civil rights movement in the 1950s and 1960s were peaceful, yet sometimes in response to aggressive police tactics a protest was recast into a violent confrontation.

Crowd Behaviour

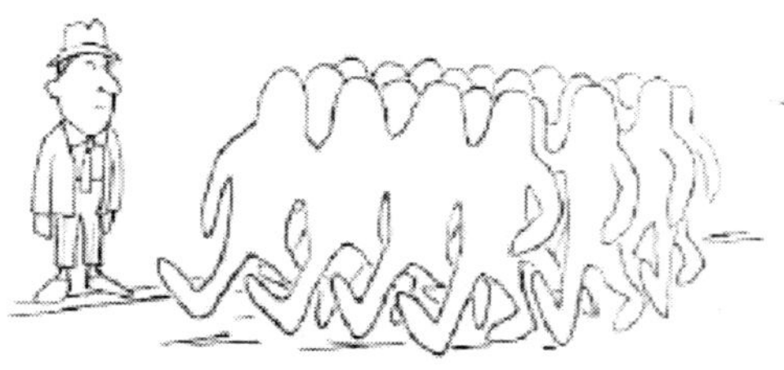

Crowds are anonymous.

A crowd is a *temporary collection of people reacting together to stimuli.* A busload of passengers, each intent upon his own interests, is not a crowd-let the driver announce that he wishes to stop for a few drinks and they may promptly become a crowd.

Unlike most other groups, a crowd is temporary. Its members rarely know "one another. Crowd behaviour is "unstructured," meaning that it has no rules, no traditions, and no formal controls, no designated leaders, no established patterns for the members to follow. Crowd behaviour may appear to be spontaneous and utterly unpredictable, but as we shall see, crowd behaviour is not purely a matter of chance or impulse. Crowd behaviour is a part of the culture. The kinds of crowds that form and the things a crowd will do and will not do differ from one culture to another. Crowd behaviour can be analyzed and understood, and to some extent predicted and controlled.

Some Characteristics of Crowd Behaviour

Anonymity

Crowds are anonymous, both because they are large and 'because' they are temporary. The size of the group and the nature of the interaction remove the sense of individuality from the members, even when they recognize acquaintances. They do not pay attention to other members as individuals and do not feel that they themselves are being singled out as individuals. Thus the restraints of a member of a crowd are reduced, and he is free to indulge in behaviour which he would ordinarily control, because moral responsibility has been shifted from him to the group. At least one study [Festinger *et al.*, 1952] claims to have confirmed these mechanisms through labouratory experimentation. Members of crowds seldom confess to any feeling of guilt after sharing in even the most outrageous atrocities, and this shift of moral responsibility to the group is part of the explanation.

Impersonality

Group behaviour is typically impersonal. The soldier bears no personal grudge against the enemy soldier he shoots, nor does it matter that the opposing football player is a personal friend. The impersonality of crowd behaviour is revealed in race riots where one member of the enemy race is as good or bad as another.

We drove around for a long time. We saw a lot of colored people, but they were in bunches. We didn't want any of that. We wanted some guy oil by himself. We saw one at Mack Avenue.

Aldo drove past him and then said, "Gimme that gun." I handed it over to him and he turned around and come back. We were about 15 feet from the man when Aldo pulled up, almost stopped and shot. The man fell and we blew.

We didn't know him. He wasn't bothering us. But other people were fighting and killing and we felt like it, too.[1]

It should be no surprise that peaceful passersby are attacked in race riots. If the other *group* is the enemy, then *any* member of the group is automatically a victim. When FLN terrorists in Algeria tossed a grenade, killing a guest in a hotel, Europeans surged into the streets and lynched the first two Moslems they found [*Time,* Aug. 11, 1961]. But if the group setting for behaviour is destroyed, then the behaviour changes. For example, in the Chicago race riot, one Negro outdistanced all but one of his assailants so that the two became separated from their groups and began to interact as individuals, whereupon they quit fighting [Chicago Commission, 1922, p. 221. Removed from their groups, they realized that fighting was pointless. Group behaviour is impersonal; when interaction becomes personal, it ceases to be group behaviour and changes in nature.

Suggestibility

Since crowd situations are normally unstructured, there are no designated leaders and no recognized behaviour patterns for the members to carry out. Furthermore their individual responsibility has been shifted to the group. Often the situation itself is confused and chaotic. In such a state of affairs, people act readily and uncritically upon suggestion, especially if the suggestion is made in a decisive, authoritative manner. The "unpredictability" of crowds is just another way of-saying that-crowds are highly suggestible [Lang and Lang, pp. 221-225].

Social Contagion

The most dramatic feature of crowd behaviour is the emotional buildup which crowd members give to one another. This com-

---

1. Alfred M. Lee and Norman D. Humphrey, *Race Riot,* Holt, Rinchart and Winston, Inc., New York, 1943, p. 88.

munication of feeling is most impressive in mobs and riots, but is found in orderly crowds as well. The first one or two cheers at a pep rally normally fall flat; not until we hear the deep swell of voices around us will we cheer very lustily. Every professional speaker or entertainer knows that an audience thinly scattered over a large auditorium will be unresponsive. A well-filled smaller hall is far better. Above all, they must be seated closely together, without many empty seats separating them. Every revivalist tries to move the audience down front so that they are close to him, and solidly packed, before he starts. The phenomenon he seeks has sometimes beer called by the cumbersome title *interactional amplification* although the term *social contagion* is simpler. This is the process where by 'the members of a crowd stimulate and respond to one another and thereby increase their emotional intensity and responsiveness. This process helps to explain why crowd behaviour sometimes goes farther than most of the members intended. A panty raid starts out as a lark; the girls protest prettily; there is a good deal of hooting, calling, and risqué kidding; matrons and administrators fuss and stew; police may try to intervene, usually without enough force to be effective; everyone gets steadily more excited as each member both stimulates and responds to every other member. Persons who came intending to be only onlookers get caught up in the process and fired themselves joining in. Sometimes the interaction reaches the riot level complete with injuries and destruction of property.

Social contagion helps to explain the great suggestibility of a crowd once it is tuned up for action A person reading in solitude a hilarious scene from a popular comedy will not find it nearly so funny as when he sees it as a member of an audience. The "claque," a small organized group that starts and leads the applause for a star at the right moment is a familiar fixture in the European opera house. Since our own actions are reinforced by the actions of others, it takes only a few to start a wave of laughter or applause.

When a crowd becomes emotionally aroused, it needs emotional release and may act upon the first suggested action which is in line with 9 impulses. Lynching mobs are not always concerned about which Negro they lynch; if the intended victim escapes, they may lynch any Negro who" is handy. In Omaha in 1919, when the mayor refused to surrender a lynch victim, the mob attempted to lynch the mayor and very nearly succeeded [*Literary Digest,* Oct. 11, 1919]. In a Texas town in 1930, the victim was hidden in the vault of the courthouse; the mob burned the courthouse then followed by wrecking the Negro part of town [Cantril, 1941, pp. 97-110]. The Civil War draft riots in New York City began as protests against the draft, but soon became full-fledged anti-Negro riots. Any suggested action, if it is in line with the established impulses and antagonisms of the members, is likely to be acted on by an emotionally aroused crowd [Lang and Lang, chap. 8].

These characteristics of crowd behaviour explain why the crowd is more than a collection of individuals. Each individual member is to some degree different in the crowd from the person he is when alone. As Allport remarks, "It used to be said in Germany that there is no such thing as a 'single Nazi.' Only with the support of a group does the peculiar subservience to the leader and his ideology take possession of the individual."[1] We can never fully understand crowd behaviour unless we understand that the crowd, like all groups, is more than merely a collection of individuals.

A crowd in action can be a terrifying thing. A factual account of everything said and done by an aggressive mob would be unprintable. To cite just one example, lynching victims were frequently burned alive, or slowly strangled, and sometimes emasculated as well as being subjected to other inexpressible

1. Gordon W. Allport in Gardner Lindzey (ed.), *Handbook of Social Psychology,* Addison-Wesley Publishing Company, Inc., Reading, Mass., 1954, vol. 1, p. 28.

tortures [Raper, 1933, pp. 6-7, 144]. People will apparently do anything when caught up in the crowd. Is this true?

Limitations on Crowd Behaviour

However irrational and unrestrained it may appear, crowd behaviour is limited" by at least four considerations: (1) the emotional needs of the members; (2) the mores of the members; (3) the leadership of the crowd; (4) the external controls over the crowd.

Emotional Needs of Members

Crowd behaviour expresses the emotional needs, resentments, and prejudices of the members. In a crowd situation people may do things they ordinarily would not do, but a crowd does only those things that most of its members *would like to do.* The emotional stimulus and protection of the crowd enables its members to express the impulses, hostilities, aggressions, and rages which they are restrained from expressing in calmer moments. Many of us, for example, like to break things, but we must restrain the impulse. In a riot men shed restraints and can tear things up without guilt feelings. If blocked from its first objective, a mob generally shifts to another. The substitute, however, still represents the hated victim, or fulfills the frustrated wish.

Homogeneous audiences are the most responsive. Having the same interests and viewpoints, the members respond enthusiastically to the speaker. The routine political rally attracts mainly the party faithful. Its function is similar to that of a pep meeting before a football game—to arouse enthusiasm and dedication to the team. A crowd is most likely to take aggressive action when its members—share a common set of prejudices and hostilities. Persons who do not share these feelings are likely to edge backward to the fringes, while the core of the crowd is made up of like-mindec members.

A crowd does only those things that most of its members would like to do.

Analysis of members of race riots (based upon eyewitness accounts and upon police records of arrested members) shows that the active participants tend to be young, unmarried, lower-class, and economically insecure [Wad; and Davies, 1957]. A great many of them already had police records for other offenses [Lee and Humphrey, 1943, pp. 80-88]. The participants therefore are likely to be persons with few responsibilities, many frustrations, and violent race prejudices. They have bitter class hostilities, reject middle-class values, and resent being lectured at and pushed around by authorities representing the middle-class world. They happily join in any riot available, and a race riot is especially satisfying.

Mores of the Members Crowd behaviour is limited by the mores of its members. The crowd rarely if ever does anything which does not claim a measure of moral approval. Lynchings do not occur in areas where the mores of most people strongly condemn them. Lynchings occur (or used to occur) only where a large proportion of the people felt that a lynching was morally justified, even necessary, under certain circumstances. The members of the lynching party normally considered themselves public benefactors, not guilty law breakers. Even the lynching party, then, is expressing, rather than violating, the mores of the members and probably the dominant mores of the region. We note, furthermore, that while the victim may be killed, burned, and mutilated, he is never crucified, nor is his body ever eaten. The crowd's mores do not support these actions.

It is true that a crowd member may confess later that he shared in acts he realizes were morally wrong. Each person, like each group, holds a number of mutually inconsistent moral views, and at a given moment one or another of them is operative. At the time it may seem very "right" that a self-appointed delegation of students should revenge past insults by painting indelicate epigrams on the walls of a rival institution; later, in the dean's office, it is equally clear that the act was destructive, illegal, and ungentlemanly. Our mores teach us that we should be loyal to family friends, and fellow workers, and should do nothing that injures other people. When a strike is called in a vital industry, such as railroad transportation or telephone communication, should the worker loyally support his striking fellows and thereby inconvenience and possibly injure the public, or should he stay on the job and thereby injure his fellows? Rarely in a behaviour situation does the individual have only *one* applicable moral judgment? Which of one's several sets of mores will operate in a particular situation will depend largely upon the group pressures surrounding him. The function of the crowd is not to paralyze the moral judgments of its members; the function of the crowd is to isolate and neutralize some of one's moral judgments, so that certain others can find unrestrained expression. Thus a crowd is doing only those things for which the mores of the participants give considerable approval.

Crowd Leadership

The leadership profoundly affects the intensity and direction of crowd behaviour. Given a collection of frustrated, resentful people, a skillful demagogue can convert them into a vengeful mob and direct their aggression at any "enemy" who is included among their antagonisms. Likewise, a leader can sometimes calm or divert a crowd by a strategic suggestion or command. In the illustration which opens this chapter, the young man stopped a mob by reminding them that they were on church property. These people were church members, and this reminder called into operation some mores which they had forgotten.

Since most crowd behaviour is unstructured, with no designated leaders, leadership is evidently "up or grabs." Anyone may be able to assume leadership by simply calling out suggestions and commands. The most unlikely persons sometime assume leadership. In the panic of the *Lusitania* ship disaster, it was an eighteen-year-old boy under whose directions a few lifeboats were successfully filled and launched [LaPiere, 1938, p. 459]. In many crowd situations, *the* members, frustrated by confusion and uncertainty, *want* to be directed, and the first person who starts giving clear orders in an authoritative manner is likely to be followed. An impressive appearance is helpful, but the assured manner of one who knows what he is doing is essential. Let us see specifically what the crowd leader does.

1. *The leader must establish rapport:* By *rapport,* we mean a responsive trusting attentiveness such as any really successful speaker gets from his audience. This author recalls observing a war-bond rally of workers in a large factory. A visiting dignitary first gave a speech which was a model of good speech construction and delivery, spoken in Harvard accents. It was received with polite applause. Then the plant manager began by holding out two ham like paws and saying, "You guys see these hands? They didn't get that way pushing a pencil. They pushed a wheelbarrow for four years, and then they operated a drill press and a turret lathe and just about every damn machine in this place." With these few words, he established rapport. He spoke their language. Rapport is most easily established by a leader who has the same background as the members. He

senses their wants, recognizes their antagonisms, speaks their language, and can predict their reactions.

2. *The leader builds emotional tensions:* For some types of crowds (mobs, riots, some audiences) he builds up their emotional tensions by an impassioned reminder of their problems and grievances. The revivalist convicts the sinners of their sins; the leader of the lynching mob arouses the men to defend the purity of their wives and daughters; the cheerleader focuses all history on the outcome of tomorrow's game. In some kinds of crowds (the panic, some audiences) the leader need not arouse emotional tension, for it already exists; he passes directly to the next function.
3. *The leader suggests action to release the tension.* The revivalist calls for repentance; the cheerleader demands victory and" lights the bonfire; the lynch leader calls, "Let's get him!"
4. *The leader justifies the suggested action.* Seldom does a crowd respond instantly to suggestion (except perhaps in panic behaviour). Generally the leader makes some effort to justify the suggestion. The revivalist pictures the new life of release from sin; the lynch leader warns, "It'll be your daughter next!" The repetition of the suggestion and its justifications permits social contagion to continue to operate, so that tension continues to mount and the need for release of tension continues to grow.

Leadership can function either to stimulate or to restrain a crowd, or to direct crowd activity from one objective to another. Leadership' is therefore, one of the limiting factors in crowd behaviour.

External Controls

Most mob behaviour occurs in the summertime when people are normally standing around and gathering in large outdoor assemblies. Cold weather discourages mobs; so do hard thundershowers Mob behaviour is rare on army posts, where military discipline can be invoked to maintain order. Servicemen must release their tensions off the post—and do so at frequent intervals!

The principal external controls on crowd behaviour, however, are those exerted by the police. There are practically no instances of persons being lynched m spite of a really determined effort of law-enforcement official, to prevent the lynching. Most lynchings were preceded by either the open connivance of law-enforcement officials, or by their merely token resistance The virtual disappearance of lynching in recent years stems in large part not from any lack of persons who would enjoy a lynching, but from the determination of law-enforcement officials to prevent lynchings.

Within recent years police have learned a great deal about the management of crowds. A sociologist, Joseph D. Lohman 11947], has prepared a widely used handbook on the handling of potential riot situations which summarizes m simple language what social science has learned about wave of directing crowd behaviour. Among the procedures used in preventing small incidents from developing into riots are: (1) preventing crowd formation by promptly arresting and carrying off noisy troublemakers and o-de-mg the onlookers to move on; (2) meeting threatened disorder with an impressive *show of force,* bringing enough police and equipment into the area so that a *use* of force is unnecessary; (3) isolating a not area by throwing a police cordon around it and allowing people to leave but not to enter the area; (4) diminishing a crowd by directing the persons on the fringes to "break up and go home," thus stripping the crowd down to its core and depriving the core of its mass support; (5) emphasis in police training on the officer's duty to maintain the peace, so that the officer s own prejudices do not lead him into the fatal error of ignoring, attacks on those whom he doesn't like.

With very few exceptions, serious riots are evidence of police failure. Recent school-integration disorders are an example. Where local police and public officials let it be known that no disorders would be tolerated, practically no disorders occurred. Where officials showed no such determination, or even invited violence by prophesying it, as did Arkansas' Governor Faubus violence developed [Blossom, 1959].

Some exceptions must be made to the proposition that police can control crowds if they wish. Small cities have no police reserves that can be shifted from place to place in an emergency. Police in a college town, outnumbered a hundred to one, may be unable to handle a student body on a rampage A local festival or celebration may bring people into a locality in numbers beyond the capacity of the police to control. Under most circumstances, however, mobs and riots in American society are symptoms of police failure.

Some Forms of Crowd Behaviour

The Audience

An audience is a crowd with interest centered on stimuli outside themselves. The stimuli are mainly one-way. With the movie, "radio or TV audience, the stimuli are entirely one-way. Every instructor however, realizes that any performer before a "live" audience is affected by the audience reaction. Dollard tells how he was stimulated by the responsive audience in a lower-class Southern Negro church which he was invited to address:

It was all I had expected and more too. Not family enough with the Bible to choose an opportunities. I talked about my own state. described the country through which I had passed in coming south, spoke of the beauty of their landed expressed my pleasure at being allowed to participate in their exercise,. Helped by appreciative murmur, which began slowly and softly and became louder and fuller as I went on. I felt a great sense of elation, an increased fluency, and a vastly expanded confidence in speaking. There was no doubt that the audience was with me, was determined to aid me in every way. I went on....

The crowd had enabled me to talk to them much more sincerely than I thought I knew how to do; the continuous surge of affirmation was a highly elating experience. For once I did no. feel that I was merely beating a sodden audience with words or striving for cold intellectual communication...

Mine was a miserable performance compared to the many Negro preachers I have seen striding the platform like confident panthers; but it was exactly the intensive collective participation that I had imagined might be. No less with the speaker than with the audience there is a sense of losing the limitations of sell and of unconscious powers rising to meet the unbound, unconscious forces of the group.[1]

Within an audience, then, there may be significant two-way stimulus and response, even though the audience situation discourages the communication. There is also a certain amount of communication between members, as they cheer, applaud, boo, whisper, mutter, doze, or snore Social contagion still operates, although at a more subdued level than in other crowds—highly subdued at a sedate church service, more freely expressive at a political rally or a sports event.

The mob: A *mob* is an emotionally aroused crowd taking aggressive action. There are several types of mobs, differing in important respects.

---

1. John Dollard, *Caste and Class in a Southern Town.* Yale University Press, New Haven, Conn., 1937, pp. 242–43.

1. The Lynching Mob

Lynching were once popular in the South and the West, although they have occurred in all parts of the country. Unlike the not, a lynching is a peculiarly American institution, rare in other parts of the world. It is a part of the vigilante tradition, wherein a self-appointed group of citizens seeks to preserve public order by punishing culprits The nineteenth-century victims were both white and Negro; twentieth-century victims became predominantly Negro; 1,795 American Negroes and 195 whites have been lynched since 1900.

Lynchings were not all alike. Raper p. 1933, pp. 55f.], and Cantril [1941, pp. 93-110] have distinguished between what they call the Bourbon and the proletarian lynching. The Bourbon lynching "took place in Deep South areas of heavy Negro population. Rigid segregation prevented direct competition between whites and Negroes, and the "poor whites" were less likely to see the Negroes as a threat and to harbor a general bitterness toward Negroes than in some other areas. A lynching was considered a deserved punishment of a specific person for a specific offense It was carried out by leading citizens (or with their encouragement; and without serious interference from law-enforcement officials. The mob was small and orderly, as though conducting a legal execution. Other Negroes were no-molested, nor was Negro property destroyed.

The proletarian lynching took place where Negroes were less numerous and then status less exactly defined. There was more "direct competition between Negroes and poor whites and much more poor-white hostility against Negroes in general. The lynching was an outburst of white antagonism against the Negro group; its object was to punish the race not just an individual. The lynching mob was large and emotional, made up mainly of poor whites, who were unconcerned with whether the victim was guilty or whether they had the right person. The lynching was generally accompanied by torture and mutilation and often followed by mistreatment of other Negroes and destruction of

Negro property. Community reaction tended to vary with social class; upper-class members and community leaders disapproved; lower-class members justified the lynching as necessary to keep the Negroes in "their place." A lynching, then, may be a pseudolegal execution by community leaders, an impassioned emotional outburst of deprived whites against the Negro race, or some combination of both. In either case the individual lyncher is supported by the crowd in taking an action which is basically in accord with his mores.

Lynching today has virtually ceased; only six persons (one white and five Negroes) were lynched during the 1950s. Although now presumably ended, lynching remains of interest to social scientists as a dramatic form of group behaviour.

2. The Riot

A riot is a violently aggressive, destructive mob. It may be a race riot, in which members of two races indiscriminately hunt down and beat or kill one another, as in Chicago in 1919 [Chicago Commission, 1922] or in Detroit in 1941 [Lee and Humphrey, 1943]. It may be a religious riot, as that between the Hindus and the Moslems in India in 1947 [Duncan, 1947; McGinty, 1947]. It may be a nationality riot, like that between American servicemen and Mexicans in Los Angeles in 1943, or the so-called "zoot-suit" riot [Turner and Surace, 1956], or the many mob actions against European immigrants in the United States during the nineteenth and early twentieth centuries [Higharn, 1955]. Race, religion, or nationality—no matter what the cause, the crowd behaviour is much the same. A group is disliked because it is different; or it serves as a convenient scapegoat; or it is hated because it threatens competition. With suitable stimulating incidents and without effective police discouragement, persons who are individually frustrated and insecure start action; it builds and grows; the attacked group strikes back, and the riot is under way.

There are other kinds of riots. The protest riot, common in colonial countries, has the object of dramatizing grievances and wringing concessions from the governing powers. The acquisitive riot is an orgy of looting and stealing. The destructive riot wrecks and burns property. In practice most riots contain elements of all these types. In the race riot in Springfield, Illinois (Lincoln's home town), in 1908, a mob of several thousand whites assaulted every Negro they could lay hands on, looted their homes and stores, and then burned the buildings [Walling, 1908]. Any riot provides the individual with the support of the crowd and a release from moral responsibility, so that he may express any impulse which seizes him. Most riots include all these elements—flaunting of authority, attack upon disliked groups, and looting and wrecking of property.

MOBS AND RIOTS

An acting crowd that becomes violent is termed a *mob, a highly emotional crowd in common pursuit of some violent or destructive goal.* Despite, or perhaps because of, their intense emotion, mobs tend to dissipate quickly. The duration of mob behaviour partly depends on whether its leadership raises or lowers the emotional intensity of the crowd, and on the mob's objectives.

Lynching is one of the most notorious examples of mob behaviour in the United States. The term "lynch" is derived from Charles Lynch, a Virginia colonist who sought to maintain law and order in his own way before formal courts were established. The word soon became synonymous with terrorism and murder outside the legal system.

After the Civil War, freed slaves gained political rights and economic opportunities, posing a threat to many whites who had previously controlled them, Especially in the South, the effort to maintain white domination sparked formation of lynch mobs, which became a highly effective form of social control. Blacks who questioned white superiority, or were even suspected of doing so, were sometimes hanged and even burned alive by vengeful whites. These blacks and occasionally their white defenders became all-purpose scapegoats.

Lynch mobs—many of Which were composed of low-status whites most threatened by black emancipation—were at a peak between 1880 and 1930: during this period about 5,000 lynchings were recorded by police. Most occurred in the Deep South, where an agrarian economy still depended on a cheap and docile black labour force, but lynchings took place in virtually every state and victimized every minority. For example, on

the western frontier, lynch mobs frequently targeted Mexican and Asian Americans. In about 25 percent of the cases, whites lynched other whites. The lynching of women, however, was rare; only about a hundred such cases are known, and almost all involved black women (White, 1969, orig. 1929; Grant, 1975).

A violent crowd without any particular purpose is a riot, *a highly emotional and undirected eruption involving violence and destruction.* Unlike a *mob* action, a not usually has no clear goal. Sometimes an apparently minor incident will trigger a not in which long-standing anger is vented (Smelser, 1962). Rioters may then indulge in seemingly random violence against property or persons. Whereas a mob action usually ends \v lien a specific violent goal has been achieved (or decisively prevented), a riot tends to disperse only when participants run out of steam or community leaders or police gradually bring them under control.

Throughout American history, riots have resulted from a collective expression of social in jus [ice. Industrial workers, for example, have rioted in outrage at their working conditions. In 1886 a bitter struggle by Chicago factory workers for an eight-hour workday led to the explosive Haymarket Riot, which left eleven dead and scores injured. Rioting born of anger and despair has also been commonplace within the American penal system. In 1987 allegedly unfair treatment by the federal government sparked rioting among Cuban prisoners in Georgia and Louisiana detention centers. Throughout American history, race riots have occurred with striking regularity. Karly in this century, crowds of whites attacked blacks in Chicago, Detroit, and oilier cities. In Los Angeles in the summer of 1965 an especially destructive riot broke out after alleged police brutality during the arrest of a black man for drunken driving, Live days of turmoil resulted in thirty-four deaths, hundreds of injuries, thousands of arrests, and millions of dollars worth of property damage, During the summers of the late 1960s, and sporadically since, riots have rocked the black ghettos of many American cities as seemingly trivial events triggered violent anger at continuing prejudice and discrimination.

Riots can also result from positive feelings, such as the high spirits characteristic of young people who flock to resort areas during college spring break. In March 1986, for example, the exuberance of vacationing students in Palm Springs, California, erupted into a riot leading to a hundred arrests after crowds of young men began throwing rocks and bottles at passing cars and stripping the clothing off terrified women (DeMott. 1986).

Chapter 8

Human Rights

HUMAN RIGHTS IN INDIA

The protection of Human Rights Act, 1993 [As amended by the Protection of Human Rights (Amendment) Act, 2006–No. 43 of 2006], National Human Rights Commission, Faridkot House, Copernicus Marg, New Delhi—110 001, Website: www.nhrc.nic.in.

The Protection of Human Rights Act, 1993[1] No. 10 of 1994 (8th January, 1994). An Act to provide for the constitution of a National Human

Rights Commission, State Human Rights Commission in States and Human Rights Courts for better protection of human rights and for matters connected therewith or incidental thereto.

Be it enacted by Parliament in the forty-fourth year of the Republic of India as follows:

Short Title, Extent and Commencement

(1) This Act may be called the Protection of Human Rights Act, 1993.

(2) It extends to the whole of India.

---

1. As amended by the Protection of Human Rights (Amendment) Act, 2006–No. 43 of 2006.

Provided that it shall apply to the State of Jammu and Kashmir only in so far as it pertains to the matters relatable to any of the entries enumerated in List I or List lll in the Seventh Schedule to the Constitution as applicable to that State.

(3) It shall be

Functions of the Commission

The Commission shall perform all or any of the following functions, namely:

(a) Inquire, suo motu or on a petition presented to it by a victim or any person on his behalf [or on a direction or order of any court]1, into complaint of (i) violation of human rights or abetment thereof;

Human Rights Courts

30. For the purpose of providing speedy trial of offences arising out of violation of human rights, the State Government may, with the concurrence of the Chief Justice of the High Court, by notification, specify for each district a Court of Session to be a Human Rights Court to try the said offences.

Provided that nothing in this section shall apply if

(a) A court of Session is already specified as a special court; or

(b) A special court is already constituted, for such offences under any other law for the time being in force.

31. Special Public Prosecutor

For every Human Rights Court, the State Government shall, by notification, specify a Public Prosecutor or appoint an advocate who has been in practice as an advocate for not less than seven years, as a Special Public Prosecutor for the purpose of conducting cases in that Court.

Amnesty International

Early on, Amnesty's founder Peter Benenson asked British artist Diana Redhouse to design an emblem for Amnesty based on a candle encircled in barbed wire. He had thought of the image when recalling a favorite proverb: "Better to light a candle than curse the darkness."

Today, the Amnesty International candle circled in barbed wire has come to be associated with everything uniquely powerful about the work of the movement and its supporters.

- The candle is the light of public attention that Amnesty members shine on the hidden abuses (the barbed wire) of human rights violators.
- The candle is the spark for dramatic, positive change—as evident in the lives of many individuals and communities, in new institutions to protect human rights, and through work to strengthen the public's awareness of our rights.
- The candle is a beacon of hope and solidarity for people who defend human rights at great personal risk, for people on death row, for the jailed and tortured and "disappeared," for people suffering the loss of "disappeared" loved ones, and for people who are forced to leave their homes in search of safe refuge in other lands.

To each person at risk of harm, Amnesty members say: "We are with you, we are telling the world about your situation, we are demanding on your behalf the justice and dignity that is your right and everyone's right."

Exposing the truth, generating change, offering hope—the Amnesty candle has become a unique symbol of people speaking out effectively for human justice and dignity in our time.

Amnesty International is a worldwide movement of people dedicated to the protection and promotion of human rights.

We are building a world in which every person enjoys the rights included in the Universal Declaration of Human Rights and other international human rights standards. Towards this end:

- Amnesty International takes action to stop grave abuses of the rights to physical and mental integrity, freedom of conscience and expression, and freedom from discrimination. We campaign, for example, to free prisoners of conscience, ensure fair trials for political prisoners, protect refugees, abolish the death penalty, end political killings, "disappearances" and torture, and bring to justice those responsible for human rights violations.
- Amnesty International seeks to expose human rights abuses accurately and quickly. We independently and impartially research and publicize the facts of individual cases and patterns of human rights abuses.
- Our members, supporters and staff then mobilize persistent public pressure on governments, armed political groups, companies and others to prevent and stop these violations.
- Amnesty International promotes public awareness and understanding of the full range of human rights, and we work with a global community of organizations to ensure broad support and respect for all human rights.
- Amnesty International is governed by its members. We are independent of all governments, political persuasions and religious creeds. We are funded by our

members and donors, and no funds are sought or accepted from governments.

People Working Together are Making a Difference

From community to community in every corner of the world, Amnesty International enables "ordinary" concerned people to work together to protect other people in danger.

Change begins each time a single, concerned person speaks out against wrongdoing.

Amnesty International helps bring together these voices of protest—giving each of us a greater power to help people to live in dignity, safety and freedom.

Amnesty members come from many cultures and backgrounds. We work in solidarity with each other, with people who become the targets of human rights abuses, and with people who defend human rights.

Amnesty International members are proud to be part of the broad, global human rights movement that includes many organizations and individuals. We often work with other groups on common concerns, and we help protect human rights defenders around the world.

Each of us—wherever we live, whoever we are—can help protect the basic human rights of everyone else, regardless of who they are, what they believe, or where they live.

Amnesty takes Effective Action for Individuals

Human rights violations are assaults against real people.

Amnesty International focuses on the lives of individual women, men and children. Our research, our campaigns, our efforts to change laws and policies, our appeals and letters—all these are aimed at affecting the lives of real individuals.

When violations take place against whole communities or on a massive scale—as they often do—Amnesty focuses public attention on this shared suffering by protecting individual victims and recounting their experiences.

We measure our effectiveness by the positive impact we have on the lives of actual people.

Amnesty Defends the Human Rights of all People Everywhere

- Human rights are the same for all people everywhere—regardless of our race, sex, sexual orientation, religion, ethnicity, political or other opinions, or national or social origin.
- Human rights are "universal": we are all born free and equal in dignity and rights.
- Human rights are "indivisible": all of us are entitled to freedom, security and a decent standard of living.
- Human rights are set out in international laws and standards which governments have a responsibility to uphold. The most widely accepted statement of these standards is the Universal Declaration of Human Rights.

Amnesty International's work is based on these agreed standards and related human rights laws. Amnesty also uses standards set out under international humanitarian law—such as the four Geneva Conventions which aim at regulating conduct during war.

Amnesty is Impartial and Independent

When Amnesty International speaks, governments feel pressured to listen.

Why? Because Amnesty International is one of the most trusted and credible voices for human rights in the world today. This credibility is due in large part to Amnesty's impartiality and independence.

"Impartiality" means that Amnesty International works for the human rights of people in every part of the world, living under all kinds of governments.

Amnesty does not support or oppose any government or political system. Amnesty does not rate countries in terms of their human rights record or their type of government. Nor does Amnesty take sides in political or armed conflicts.

Our reports are accurate, unbiased and fair—free from the influence of those in power. Our demands are based on international human rights standards, not on the interests of any government or group.

Amnesty International is able to be impartial because we are independent of any government, political belief, economic interest or religion.

Amnesty is financially independent—funded by our supporters around the world. Amnesty accepts no money from governments for its operating budgets. And Amnesty is democratic and self-governing—a movement run by Amnesty members.

Amnesty takes Effective Action in Changing Times

Amnesty International began in 1961 as an act of protest against people being held in prison because of their beliefs. Thousands of concerned people around the world set out to free these "prisoners of conscience"—and their protests were hugely successful.

Over time, Amnesty members have decided to defend other civil and political rights. For example, we began to campaign for fair trials in political cases, and against the torture of all prisoners.

In the 1970s, we decided to oppose the death penalty in all cases—and we then extended this stand to oppose political killings and "disappearances."

Amnesty International has always kept a close watch over world events—the changing threats to human rights and new opportunities to protect people's rights. And we have constantly adapted our mission and tactics in response to the se historical changes.

Sometimes, Amnesty International members and non-members have challenged Amnesty to better understand and take action against violations experienced by particular groups of people, such as women, refugees, lesbian, gay, bisexual and transgender people, and Indigenous peoples.

Out of these dialogues have come significant changes to the range of injustices on which Amnesty works, as well as the tactics we use.

For Amnesty International the most important question is this: As our world changes, what is the most effective work we can do to protect human rights?

Today, our answers to this question are taking into account new forces that are having a major impact on human rights, such as corporate globalization and renewed movements for change.

Today we are focusing our actions on some of the deepest patterns and causes of human rights abuse in our times:

- Challenging patterns of discrimination that lead to violations against women.
- Preventing mass human rights violations in the context of civil and regional conflicts.
- Stopping the global trade in arms that often intensifies these conflicts.
- Ensuring the safety of the increasing number of people seeking refuge from these conflicts.

Amnesty is Based on Democracy and Mutual Respect

Amnesty International is democratic and self-governing.

Amnesty members all over the world set Amnesty's mission, decide what major issues Amnesty should be working on, and how Amnesty should work.

Amnesty representatives from around the world gather every two years to set policy at the International Council Meeting (ICM). The Council also elects an International Executive Committee which ensures that the ICM's decisions are carried out.

Wherever Amnesty International is formally organized in a particular country, such as in Canada, Amnesty members meet regularly to set policy and elect an Executive Committee. In Canada, this executive works in partnership with staff to guide national operations during the year.

Amnesty members in each country take action on human rights cases and major campaigns shared by the international movement. Within this broad framework, members plan their own activities in schools and communities and across electronic networks.

Amnesty International's work is always being assessed by our members and staff in light of changing world circumstances. When major changes in policy and approach are needed, Amnesty members make the final decision.

Chapter 9

Mob Justice in Literature

JAMES WELDON JOHNSON, THE AUTOBIOGRAPHY OF AN EX-COLORED MAN

The fictitious *The Autobiography of an Ex-Coloured Man* (initially published anonymously in 1912), by James Weldon Johnson, narrates the travels and experiences of a Negro "passing" for a white man. In the following passage, a Negro is burned alive by a frenzied crowd.

A space was quickly cleared in the crowd, and a rope placed about his neck, when from somewhere came the suggestion, "Burn him!" It ran like an electric current. Have you ever witnessed the transformation of human beings into savage beasts? Nothing can be more terrible. A railroad tie was sunk into the ground, the rope was removed, and a chain brought and securely coiled round the victim and the stake. There he stood, a man only in form and stature, every sign of degeneracy stamped upon his countenance. His eyes were dull and vacant, indicating not a single ray of thought. Evidently the realization of his fearful fate had robbed him of whatever reasoning power he had ever possessed. He was too stunned and stupefied even to tremble. Fuel was brought from everywhere, oil, the torch; the flames crouched for an instant as though to gather strength, then leaped up as high as their victim's head. He squirmed, he writhed, strained at his chains, then gave out cries and groans that I shall always hear. The cries and groans were choked off by the fire and smoke; but his eyes, bulging from the sockets, rolled from side to side, appealing in vain for help. Some of the crowd yelled and cheered, others seemed appalled at what they had done, and there were those who turned away sickened at the sight. I was fixed to the spot where I stood, powerless to take my eyes from what I did not want to see... A great wave of humiliation and shameswept over me. Shame that I belonged to a race that could be so dealt with.

WILLIAM FAULKNER, *LIGHT IN AUGUST*

The following excerpt is from William Faulkner's 1932 novel *Light in August.* A mob watches as Percy Grimm brutally completes the lynching of Joe Christmas for the murder of his white lover with a ritual that was not uncommon in the late 19th and early 20th centuries.

They saw that the man was not dead yet, and when they saw what Grimm was doing one of the men gave a choked cry and stumbled back into the wall and began to vomit. Then Grimm too sprang back, flinging behind him the bloody butcher knife. "Now you'll let white women alone, even in hell," he said. But the man on the floor had not moved. He just lay there, with his eyes open and empty of everything save consciousness, and with something, a shadow, about his mouth. For a long moment he looked up at them with peaceful and unfathomable and unbearable eyes. Then his face, body, all, seemed to collapse, to fall in upon itself and from out the slashed garments about his hips and loins the pent black blood seemed to rush like a released breath. It seemed to rush out of his pale body like the rush of sparks from a rising rocket; upon that black blast the man seemed to rise soaring into their memories forever and ever. They are not to lose it, in whatever peaceful valleys, beside whatever placid and reassuring streams of old age, in the mirroring faces of whatever children they will contemplate old disasters and newer hopes. It will be there, musing, quiet, steadfast, not fading and not particularly threatful but of itself alone serene, of itself alone triumphant.

THOMAS DIXON JR., TWO EXCERPTS

Thomas Dixon Jr.'s *The Clansmen: A Historical Romance of the Ku Klux Klan* (1905) was, along with another Dixon novel, *The Leopard's Spots*, the basis for D. W. Griffith's film *Birth of a Nation*. Dixon was a Baptist minister, lawyer and writer from North Carolina. In this passage from *The Clansmen*, the chaplain of the Clan recites a prayer before a black murder suspect is quickly tried in the Clan's own court and then murdered.

As we wrestle with the powers of darkness now strangling our lives, give to our souls to endure as seeing the invisible, and to our right arms the strength of the martyred dead of our people. Have mercy on the poor, the weak, the innocent and defenseless, and deliver us from the body of the Black Death. In a land of light and beauty and love our women are prisoners of danger and fear. While the heathen walks his native heath unharmed and unafraid, in this fair Christian Southland, our sisters, wives, and daughters dare not stroll at twilight through the streets, or step beyond the highway at noon. The terror of the twilight deepens with the darkness, and the stoutest heart grows sick with fear for the red message the morning bring.

Despite his beliefs in white superiority and his high esteem for the Ku Klux Klan, even Dixon could step back and examine the maniacal savagery of the lynch mob. In *The Leopard's Spots* (1902), a white man tries to intervene in a lynching only to be forced into watching.

He stood in helpless rage and pity, and as he saw the match applied, bowed his head and burst into tears. He looked up at the silent crowd standing there like voiceless ghosts with renewed wonder. Under the glare of the light and the tears the crowd seemed to melt into a great crawling swaying creature, half reptile half beast, half dragon half man, with a thousand legs, and a thousand eyes, and ten thousand gleaming teeth, and with no ear to hear and no heart to pity!

JEAN TOOMER, TWO EXCERPTS

Portrait in Georgia

In his 1923 poem "Portrait in Georgia," Jean Toomer subverts categories of race and gender as a white woman is transformed into a black lynching victim.

Hair-braided chestnut,
coiled like a lyncher's rope,
Eyes—fagots,
Lips—old scars, or the first red blisters,
Breath—the last sweet scent of cane,
And her slim body, white as the ash
of black flesh after flame.
Cane

When Jean Toomer visited Sparta, Georgia in 1921, echoes of the gruesome lynching of Mary Turner and the rash of eleven other lynchings that followed were still resonating, surrounding the black population of the nearby areas in a haze of fear and paranoia. It was in this setting that Toomer composed a collection of stories that comprised the novel *Cane*. In one of these stories, "Kabnis," an NAACP report's account of Mary Turner is recreated with few alterations, depicting the brutal execution of Mame Lamkins at the hands of a lynch mob.

They killed her in the street, an some white man see in the risen in her stomach as she lay there soppy in her blood like any cow, took an ripped her belly open, an the kid fell out. It was living, but a nigger baby aunt supposed t live. So he jabbed his knife in it a stuck it t a tree. A then they all went away.

THOMAS NELSON PAGE, "THE NEGRO: THE SOUTHERNER'S PROBLEM"

A contemporary and friend of Thomas Dixon, Thomas Nelson Page dealt with the morality of lynching by acquitting the mob from any guilt, holding, instead, the supposedly debased Negroes responsible for their own violent executions. The following excerpts are taken from Page's essay, "The Negro: The Southerner's Problem," published in 1904.

Lynching does not end ravishing, and that is the prime necessity...

The charge that is often made, that the innocent are sometimes lynched, has little foundation. The rage of a mob is not directed against the innocent, but against the guilty; and its fury would not be satisfied with any other sacrifices than the death of the real criminal. Nor does the criminal merit any consideration, however terrible the punishment. The real injury is to the perpetrators of the crime of destroying the law, and to the community in which the law is slain...

The crime of lynching is not likely to cease until the crime of ravishing and murdering women and children is less frequent than it has been of late. And this crime, which is well-nigh wholly confined to the Negro race, will not greatly diminish until the Negroes themselves take it in hand and stamp it out...

As the crime of rape of late years had its baleful renascence in the teaching of equality and the placing of power in the ignorant Negroes' hands, so its perpetuation and increase have undoubtedly been due in large part to the same teaching. The intelligent Negro may understand what social equality truly means, but to the ignorant and brutal young Negro, it signifies but one thing: the opportunity to enjoy, equally with white men, the privilege of cohabiting with white women.

MARK TWAIN, TWO EXCERPTS

Perhaps the most famous literary foe of lynching as a practice, Mark Twain invoked powerful words numerous times throughout his career to fight what he called "the epidemic of bloody insanities." Twain's most forceful and direct attack against lynching came in his essay "The United States of Lyncherdom" (1901) in which he called upon American missionaries in China to return home and fight native savagery.

[We ask them to] picture the scene in their minds, and soberly ponder it; then multiply it by 115, add 88; place the 203 in a row, allowing 600 feet of space for each human torch, so that there may be viewing room around it for 5,000 Christian American men, women, and children, youths and maidens; make it night, for grim effect; have the show in a gradually rising plain, and let the course of the stakes be uphill; the eye can then take in the whole line of twenty-four miles of blood and flesh bonfires unbroken....

All being ready now, and the darkness opaque, the stillness impressive for there should be no sound but the soft moaning of the night wind and the muffled sobbing of the sacrifices; let all the far stretch of kerosened pyres be touched off simultaneously and the glare and the shrieks and the agonies burst heavenward to the Throne.

Twain's brief essay *Only a Nigger* appeared anonymously in the Buffalo Express on August 26, 1869, as one of his earliest and most ironic protests against lynching.

Mistakes will happen, even in the conduct of the best regulated and most high-toned mobs, and surely there is no good reason why Southern gentlemen should worry themselves with useless regrets, so long as only an innocent "nigger" is hanged, or roasted or knouted to death, now and then...

Keep the lash knotted; keep the brand and the faggots in waiting, for prompt work with the next "nigger" who may be suspected of any damnable crime! Wreak a swift vengeance upon him, for the satisfaction of the noble impulses that animate knightly hearts, and then leave time and accident to discover, if they will, whether he was guilty or no.

Richard Wright, "Between the World and Me"

Lynching profoundly affected the work of Richard Wright. He used the ritualized burnings, as Trudier Harris put it, "to shape the basis of his aesthetic visions of the world," and his 1935 poem "Between the World and Me" is a testament to the power of these visions.

And one morning while in the woods I stumbled
suddenly upon the thing,
Stumbled upon it in a grassy clearing guarded by scaly
oaks and elms
And the sooty details of the scene rose, thrusting
themselves between the world and me....
There was a design of white bones slumbering forgottenly
upon a cushion of ashes.
There was a charred stump of a sapling pointing a blunt
finger accusingly at the sky.
There were torn tree limbs, tiny veins of burnt leaves, and
a scorched coil of greasy hemp;
A vacant shoe, an empty tie, a ripped shirt, a lonely hat,
and a pair of trousers stiff with black blood.
And upon the trampled grass were buttons, dead matches,
butt-ends of cigars and cigarettes, peanut shells, a
drained gin-flask, and a whore's lipstick;
Scattered traces of tar, restless arrays of feathers, and the
lingering smell of gasoline.
And through the morning air the sun poured yellow
surprise into the eye sockets of the stony skull....

And while I stood my mind was frozen within cold pity
for the life that was gone.
The ground gripped my feet and my heart was circled by
icy walls of fear—
The sun died in the sky; a night wind muttered in the
grass and fumbled the leaves in the trees; the woods
poured forth the hungry yelping of hounds; the
darkness screamed with thirsty voices; and the witnesses rose and lived:
The dry bones stirred, rattled, lifted, melting themselves
into my bones.
The grey ashes formed flesh firm and black, entering into
my flesh.
The gin-flask passed from mouth to mouth, cigars and
cigarettes glowed, the whore smeared lipstick red
upon her lips,
And a thousand faces swirled around me, clamoring that
my life be burned....
And then they had me, stripped me, battering my teeth
into my throat till I swallowed my own blood.
My voice was drowned in the roar of their voices, and my
black wet body slipped and rolled in their hands as
they bound me to the sapling.
And my skin clung to the bubbling hot tar, falling from
me in limp patches.
And the down and quills of the white feathers sank into
my raw flesh, and I moaned in my agony.
Then my blood was cooled mercifully, cooled by a
baptism of gasoline.

And in a blaze of red I leaped to the sky as pain rose like water, boiling my limbs

Panting, begging I clutched childlike, clutched to the hot sides of death.

Now I am dry bones and my face a stony skull staring in yellow surprise at the sun....

MAYA ANGELOU, I KNOW WHY THE CAGED BIRD SINGS

Poet, playwright, and actor Maya Angelou recounts growing up in St. Louis, Missouri and Stamps, Arkansas in the 1930s and 40s in her autobiography, *I Know Why the Caged Bird Sings* (1970). As a youth, she attends a boxing match between a white boxer and a black boxer, Joe Louis. When the contender knocks Louis out, she says,

My race groaned. It was our people falling. It was another lynching, yet another Black man hanging on a tree. One more woman ambushed and raped. A Black boy whipped and maimed. It was hounds on the trail of a man running through slimy swamps. It was a white woman slapping her maid for being forgetful.

LEWIS ALLAN, *STRANGE FRUIT*

These 12 lines form one of literature's most powerful and moving attacks on lynching. The poem was written and set to a haunting, blues melody by a white, Jewish school teacher from New York City named Abel Meeropol, who wrote under the pseudonym Lewis Allan. Billie Holiday began performing the song in early 1939 and ever since, *Strange Fruit* has been synonymous with lynched victims.

Southern trees bear a strange fruit blood on the leaves and blood at the root Black boy swinging' in the Southern breeze Strange fruit hanging from the poplar trees

Pastoral scene of the gallant South. The bulging eyes and the twisted mouth Scent of magnolia sweet and fresh And the sudden smell of burning flesh

Here is a fruit for the crows to pluck

For the rain to gather, for the wind to suck For the sun to rot, for the tree to drop Here is a strange and bitter crop.

LORRAINE HANSBERRY, *LYNCHSONG*

At age 21, eight years before she won national recognition for her now-classic play *A Raisin in the Sun*, playwright Lorraine Hansberry wrote "Lynchsong." The 1951 poem reads as a faint sketch from memory-images and thoughts form a rough document of some painful, past recollection.

I can hear Rosalee
See the eyes of Willie McGee
My mother told me about
Lynchings
My mother told me about
The dark nights
And dirt roads
And torch lights
And lynch robes

The
faces of men
Laughing white
Faces of men
Dead in the night
sorrow night
and a
sorrow night

RALPH ELLISON, *THE BIRTHMARK*

The Birthmark first appeared in the left-wing magazine *New Masses* in 1940, a time when Ralph Ellison was under the tutelage of RichardWright. Early in the story, Matt must identify the body of his brother, While, who was ostensibly hit by a car. Matt finds the body mutilated-lynched.

When Matt lowered his eyes he noticed the ribs had been caved in. The flesh was bruised and torn. The birthmark was just below Willie's navel, he thought. Then he gave a start: where it should have been was only a bloody mound of torn flesh and hair. Matt went weak. He felt as though he had been castrated himself...

"Just remember that a car hit 'im, and you'll be all right," the patrolman said. "We don't allow no lynching round here no more."

DAN PARKINSON, *THE PRODIGAL*

Texan journalist and fiction writer Dan Parkinson's short story The Prodigal appears in the anthology *New Frontiers Vol. 1* (1990). In this dark, mystical account, two strangers intervene in a poorly executed lynching in bleak Jenk's Hole.

In the first place, that loop on his neck. Can't anybody here tie a proper knot? And no slack. You won't break his neck. He'll just strangle.

LEWIS D. PATTEN, *NO GOD IN SAGUARO*

Lewis D. Patten explored the issue of guilt associated with lynching through Western novels in the 1960s and 70s. In *No God in Saguaro* (1966), what appeared to be "just another lynching" resulted in the town destroying itself because of its guilty conscience. The town judge, one of the perpetrators, explains what compelled him to irrationally join the lynch mob.

I joined that mob six months ago in spite of my training in the law, in spite of the fact that everything I had been taught abhorred mob violence. I joined it in a moment of passion, in a moment of blind fury because I had lost something." His mouth twisted ruefully.

"... Something I'd never even had."

In Patten's 1974 *Lynching at Broken Butte*, a judge incites a mob to avenge the murder of his daughter. The legacy of the lynching results in the demise of the town. He falsely accuses two drifting cowboys and encourages the lynch mob to kill them.

Carberry yelled, "Have one more drink! Then one of you get a couple of ropes and we'll go across the street and get those sonsabitches out of jail. There's that big cottonwood down by the livery barn. We'll string 'em up to it.". The liquor they had consumed and the excitement now had its grip on them. They shoved him angrily aside when he got in their way. They threw the ropes over the horizontal cottonwood branch, and put hangman's nooses in their ends. They boosted the prisoners bodily onto the horses after they tied their hands behind their backs. A man mounted a third horse and put the nooses over the prisoners' heads. The ends were tied.

JOHN HOWARD GRIFFIN, *BLACK LIKE ME*

In *Black Like Me* (1960), John Howard Griffin darkened his skin to discover the black experience in the Deep South. He came across Louisiana's Negro newspaper, which condemned the Mack Charles Parker lynching of the previous year, offering a contemporary black perspective on lynching.

If there was any doubt as to how "Southern Justice" operates in the State of Mississippi, it was completely dispelled. when the Pearl River County Grand Jury failed to return any indictments or even consider the massive information compiled by the FBI in the sensational Mack Parker kidnap-lynch murder case. The axiom that a man is innocent until guilty by a court of law has been flagrantly ignored once again in the State of Mississippi. The fact that an accused man was deprived of a fair trial, kidnapped and murdered by a lynch mob from a Mississippi jail apparently had no effect on the thinking of the Grand Jury. The silent treatment merely gave approval of the mob taking the law into its hands. Mississippi has long had a reputation of failing to punish white men accused of criminal acts against Negroes. This is Mississippi's peculiar way of making Negroes "happy and contented" with the democratic processes and of showing the world how well they care for the Negro in respecting his rights as an American citizen.

WALTER WHITE, WHY I REMAIN A NEGRO

In *Why I Remain a Negro*, Walter White, president of the National Association for the Advancement of Colored Peoples (NAACP) explains his anger and pride concerning the black condition. He remembers an attempted lynching.

I heard a voice cry out, a voice which I knew belonged to the son of our neighborhood grocer. "Let's burn the house of the nigger mail carrier! It's too nice a house for a nigger to live in!" I knew then who I was. I was colored, a human being with an invisible pigmentation which marked me a person to be hunted, hanged, abused, discriminated against, kept in poverty and ignorance, in order that those whose skin was white would have readily at hand a proof to their superiority, a proof patent and inclusive, accessible to the moron and the idiot as well as to the wise man and the genius.

LYNCHING BALLADS

The ballad of J.V. Johnson takes a definitive stance against lynching. The mob is accused of disobeying the laws of God and Johnson receives the final word in which he pitifully contemplates the fate of his soul. The ballad acknowledges

Johnson's guilt and the severity of his crime while still refusing to romanticize his punishment.

J.V. JOHNSONS

'T was on a gloomy Sunday night
When Johnson thought he was alright
A hundred hearts of an angry mob
Did disobey the laws of God
'T was on land [?] at half past two.
The great fair [?] doors the men broke through.
They scarcely [?] for this poor man.
The cell was opened at their command.
Into the cell they boldly went,
And only there a moment spent.
"Come out, come out, your time has come
When you'll repay the deed you've done."
"Don't hurt me boys," he sadly said.
"Hush, hush your mouth you'll soon be dead."
"Oh just give me one moment to pray,
And do not kill a man who prays."
"You did not give Guinn time to pray.
You took his dear sweet life away."
We will not give you time to pray,
But for his life your life shall pay."
That was a sad and awful time.
Just as they reached the fatal time.
A rope around his neck they tied,
And hung the man until he died.
"I know this crime is awful black.

I wish that I could call it back.

It is so dark I cannot see.

My soul, what will become of thee?"

"Farewell, this world, my friends, my wife.

This mob will surely take my life.

It is so dark I cannot see.

My soul, what will become of thee?"

The Lynching Ballads of Alec Whitley Written to commemorate the 1892 lynching of Alec Whitley, the first ballad was composed before he was actually killed and consequently deals most specifically with a crime, the murder of Burt Tucker, that would eventually lead to Whitley's lynching. The victim's case involves a white man lynched by a white mob. Written by a Baptist Minister, Rev. Edmond P. Harrington, it has been suggested that Harrington sold copies of the ballad to be sung at Whitley's spectacle lynching. This practice was somewhat widespread as the composer could earn a tidy sum by exploiting the festive atmosphere common to many lynchings of that era. The seventh stanza, excerpted below, shows Alec's half-sister warning him of his impending fate.

The ballad "Alec Whitley" was most probably written to preserve the history of the same lynching. It is a fairly straightforward account and an interesting portrait of the town's emotional climate expressing satisfaction with the execution.

Alec Whitley

They hung Alec Whitley to a red oak limb,

They hung Alec Whitley to a red oak limb,

They hung Alec Whitley to a red oak limb,

Just to show the world what they'd do for him. Stanza 4

Lines Written on the Assassination of D. B. Tucker

Judy says, "Oh, Alec, you'll die in public sure,

For murdering Cousin Burton, and mangling his body so.

You'll be arrested for this, and in the jail you'll go

And on the fatal hangman's tree, you'll pay the debt you owe." Stanza 7

ALAN TATE, "THE SWIMMERS"

The Allen Tate poem, "The Swimmers" evokes images of water amid shady slopes in rural Montgomery County, Kentucky—in the aftermath of a lynching. Set in July 1911 when Tate himself was twelve years old (born 1899, he died in 1979), it describes a boy and his friends watching the corpse of a lynched man drifting down a river as three dark and brutal figures disappear into a nearby clearing. These events, as depicted in the poem, affect the boys drastically, probably traumatizing them for the rest of their lives. Published singly in 1953 (and seventeen years later as part of a collection), "The Swimmers" remains one of Tate's most evocative works.

Kentucky water, clear springs: a boy fleeing

To water under the dry Kentucky sun,

His four little friends in tandem with him, seeing

Long shadows of grapevine wriggle and run

Over the green swirl; mullein under the ear

Soft as Nausicaa's palm; sullen fun

Savage as childhood's thin harmonious tear:

O fountain, bosom source undying-dead

Replenish me the spring of love and fear

And give me back the eye that looked and fled

When a thrush idling in the tulip tree

Unwound the cold dream of the copperhead.

Along the creek the road was winding; we

Felt the quicksilver sky. I see again

The shrill companions of that odyssey:
Bill Eaton, Charlie Watson, "Nigger" Layne
The doctor's son, Harry Duesler who played
The flute; and Tate, with water on the brain.
Dog-days; the dusty leaves where rain delayed
Hung low on poison-oak and scuppernong,
And we were following the active shade
Of water, that bells and bickers all night long.
"No more'n a mile," Layne said. All five stood still.
Listening, I heard what seemed at first a song;
Peering, I heard the hooves come down the hill.
The posse passed, twelve horse; the leader's face
Was worn as limestone on an ancient sill.
Then, as sleepwalkers shift from a hard place
In bed, and rising to keep a formal pledge
Descend a ladder into empty space,
We scuttled down the bank below a ledge
And marched stiff-legged in our common fright
Along a hog-track by the riffle's edge;
Into a world where sound shaded the sight
Dropped the dull hooves again; the horsemen came
Again, all but the leader. It was night
Momently and I feared: eleven same
Jesus-Christers unmembered and unmade,
Whose corpse had died again in dirty shame.
The bank then levelling in a specked glade,
We stopped to breathe above the swimming hole;
I gazed at its reticulated shade
Recoiling in blue fear, and felt it roll

Over my ears and eyes and lift my hair
Like seaweed tossing on a sunk atoll.
I rose again. Borne on the copper air,
A distant voice green as a funeral wreath
Against a grave: "That dead nigger there."
The melancholy sheriff slouched beneath
A giant sycamore; shaking his head
He plucked a sassagras twig and picked his teeth:
"We come too late." He spoke to the tired dead
Whose ragged shirt soaked up the viscous flow
Of blood in which It lay discomfited.
A butting horse-fly gave one ear a blow
And glanced off, as the sheriff kicked the rope
Loose from the neck and hooked it with his toe
Away from the blood.—I looked back down the slope:
The friends were gone that I had hoped to greet.—
A single horseman came at a slow lope
And pulled up at the hanged man's horny feet;
The sheriff noosed the feet, the other end
The stranger tied to his pommel in a near
Slip-knot. I saw the Negro's body bend
And straighten, as a fish-line cast transverse
Yields to the current that it must subtend.
The Sheriff's Goddamn was a murmured curse
Not for the dead but for the blinding dust
That boxed the cortege in a cloudy hearse
And dragged it towards our town. I knew I must
Not stay till twilight in that silent road;
Sliding my bare feet into the warm crust,

I hopped the stonecrop like a panting toad
Mouth open, following the heaving cloud
That floated to the court-house square its load
Of limber corpse that took the sun for shroud.
There were three fingers in the dying sun
Whose light were company where three was crowd.
My breath crackled the dead air like a shotgun
As, sheriff and the stranger disappearing,
The faceless head lay still. I could not run
Or walk, but stood. Alone in the public clearing
This private thing was owned by all the town,
Though never claimed by us within my hearing.

Incidence of Lynching in Mississippi 1865-1890 as a Function of the Severity of Civil War Damages

RICHARD B. STEVENS

The term Lynch law has been traced to the American Revolution and a Virginia Quaker named Charles Lynch. During the years of revolt, cattle thieves and other bandits took advantage of the confused state of affairs. Faced with a criminal court more than 200 miles away, Lynch and others formed their own court, with Lynch as chief judge. "The accused was faced with his accusers, permitted to give testimony, and allowed to summon witnesses, and in every possible way his rights were safeguarded." This description of frontier justice, and justice it seems to be, is a far cry from the torture and barbarity that accompanied what later came to be called lynching. As the incidence and cruelty of lynching increased during and after Reconstruction, interest in the prevention and causes of lynching grew.

The South suffered drastic economic and political changes during the mid-Nineteenth Century. The southern economy shifted from pre—Civil War emphasis on a slave labour based cotton economy to an arguably free labour based cotton economy. This shift added to the physical damages inherent in any war zone, made a shambles of what had been a booming agricultural economy. In Mississippi over a space of less than thirty years political power shifted from the control of a relatively few wealthy men to the federal authorities and back again. This political power shift was accompanied by changes in the legal structure of the state government through both legal and extralegal means. Extralegal means, especially terrorism and lynching have become so strongly associated with the South that this stigma exists even today. Could it be that there was a link between the economic disaster of war and reconstruction and the incidence of lynching in the years between 1865 and 1890? Did the amount of damage inflicted by the war cause an increase in the number of post war lynchings? A preliminary county by county analysis of lynching incidence and property values in Mississippi seems to indicate that there is such a link if not causation.

The Civil War fought in the United States from 1861to 1865 has the distinction of being one of three wars fought inside the boundaries of the United States. It is the only war in which for a period of time afterward an occupying army imposed a system of military rule on a part of the country. After the war a period of Radical Reconstruction occurred during which local rule in the South was replaced by government imposed at the national level.

Lynching, like most actions, was not distributed equally across the South nor was the practice distributed equally across Mississippi. Some counties had no lynchings in the thirty-five years immediately after the war while in others lynching seemed to be a fairly common occurrence. In Hinds County, for example, there were seventeen recorded lynchings between 1865 and 1890 when the Redeemers in Mississippi adopted a new state constitution.

John Dollard argued in 1937 that lynching was a means of maintaining white supremacy in the South. Later work began to include hints of the relationship between race and sex on lynching. W. J. Cash presented and defended the image of the black beast rapist and how this idea, coupled with the ideal of the purity of southern womanhood, did indeed contribute to the underlying causes of lynching in the South. Joel Williamson suggested there was a symbolic aspect to lynching; that "black men were lynched for having achieved, seemingly, a sexual liberation that white men wanted but could not achieve without great feelings of guilt... the black man lynched was the worst part of [white men]."

In the popular culture, rape of a white woman by a black man was widely reported as a cause for lynching, however, this idea was being questioned as early as the 1920's. Walter White wrote in 1929 that since 1881, 92 women had been lynched in America. While it is possible that all these women were accused of rape, it seems highly unlikely. According to Jan Hillegas of New Mississippi, Inc. in cases where the charge against the lynching victim is known from 1865 to 1890 there were 102 lynchings in which the victim was charged with murder. In the same period according to the same study, 74 lynched people were accused of rape or attempted rape. Although from a later period, from 1889 to 1932, 1406 lynching victims were accused of homicide, while only 878 were accused of rape or attempted rape. According to these studies, rape or attempted rape does not seem to stand up as a causative factor for lynching, and that the threat of rape in fact did not exist as a reasonable fear.

Lynching has been a subject of inquiry since before 1900 and since that time has been subjected to numerical and statistical analysis. Analysis for economic linkage, if not causation, was done as early as the 1930's. Raper cited a study done by T. J. Woofter, Jr. for the Southern Commission on the Study of Lynching which seemed to link the total number of lynchings in the United States to the value of cotton per acre.

Woofter found that during the years 1900 to 1930 the incidence of lynching seemed to decrease as the dollar value of cotton per acre rose. In other words, when cotton land was more valuable, fewer people were lynched. However, Woofter does not report considering other variables, nor does his study take into account the local variations in lynching rates that Brundage described.

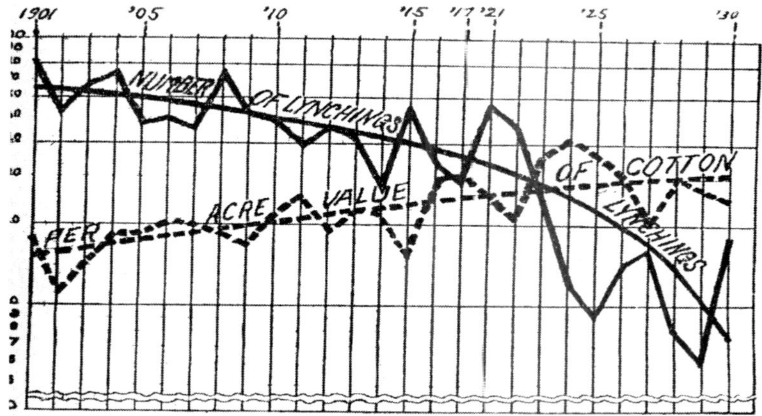

Figure 1 Comparison of lynching incidence to dollar value per acre of cotton, 1900-1931. (Woofter, in Raper, *The Tragedy of Lynching*, p. 31.

In 1967 Hubert Blalock expressed what has become known as the power threat hypothesis of lynching. He proposed that lynching was an expression of political concerns, not sexual or morality based ideologies. Blalock stated that Lynching was used by whites as a means of controlling the black population through terror and intimidation. He predicted that lynching rates would be higher in counties with a larger percentage black population.

John Shelton Reed tested this hypothesis using a grouping of Mississippi counties as his test field. Reed argues that Blalock's hypothesis does hold up for Mississippi under statistical analysis. However, Reed also found that the trends he found for Mississippi (that lynching incidence increases as the percentage of black population increases) did not hold for similar studies in Arkansas and South Carolina. Apparently, Reed either did not take the proper variables into account or other influences were not examined completely.

Later analysis by Corzine, Creech and Corzine supported Blalock's and Reed's findings. Corzine extended the study of lynching outside the Deep South in an attempt to explore Reed's statements that Blalock's findings were not applicable in all cases. Corzine included variables for rural and urban population percentages and illiteracy rates.

In a contrary vein, analysis by Stewart Tolnay and others contradicts the findings of Blalock, Reed, and Corzine. In an effort to further correct for perceived problems with sampling and an inappropriate measure of lynching Tolnay re-examined the data and analysis of the previous authors and concluded that the assertions of Blalock, Reed, and Corzine were unsupported by the evidence. In one of the most interesting exchanges of academic opinions in recent publication, all three previous authors were allowed to respond to Tolnay's assertions. All three remain overwhelmingly unconvinced of Tolnay's accuracy.

Anecdotal evidence in support of the Power Threat hypothesis does exist. One extralegal means of gaining and maintaining power was the use of terror by organized groups such as the Ku Klux Klan. Although the Ku Klux Klan was not responsible for every lynching in Mississippi during reconstruction the rise in the incidence of lynching after the Civil War, and especially the shift toward mostly black victims coincides with the establishment and rise of the Klan during Reconstruction. Established in Pulaski, Tennessee in 1865 the Klan rose to such strength that Congress felt compelled to pass the Force Act (1870) and the Ku Klux Act (1871) to combat the Klan. Speaking of the relationship of the Freedmen to the Ku Klux Klan, one West Alabama planter recalled that "Had it not been for their deadly fear of the Ku Klux, I do not think we could have managed them as well as we did."

Fitzhugh Brundage cautioned against psychological motivations and interpretations of lynching until at least such time as more is known about family and personal life in the South during the Post Bellum era. He also pointed out that psychological explanations failed to account for temporal and regional differences in both the incidence and the barbarity of lynching. "Distinctive conditions, not some rigid notion of white supremacy, explain why mobs executed more blacks in central Georgia than in the low country of South Carolina."

Methodology and Findings

Lynching has been recorded in Mississippi as early as 1800. Although initially lynching seems to be an equal opportunity mode of extralegal execution during and immediately after Radical Reconstruction it became an overwhelmingly black dominated institution. Of 72 instances of Mississippi lynching recorded by Jan Hillegas between 1800 and 1864, 38 victims were white, 33 were black, and the race of one victim is not known. In the years from 1865 to 1890, black lynching victims far outnumbered their white counterparts. Of the 268 people Hillegas reported were lynched in Mississippi during the 35 years immediately after the Civil War, 221 were black, 35 were white, and the race of 12 is not known. Any summary of lynchings that claims to be complete, a claim Hillegas does not make, should be suspect. Hillegas study was chosen because it focused only on Mississippi, was readily accessible, and presented a different data pool from that used by Blalock and Reed.

First, an attempt to replicate the findings of Blalock and Reed was attempted. Reed using a calculated figure derived from the percentage of black population in a given county from the 1910 and using lynching figures from 1890 to 1930 census to calculate a lynching rate per 1000 black population. Both Reed and Blalock reported a positive correlation for these numbers. A similar result was found for the years 1865 to 1890 using population figures from the 1870 census and the lynching figures reported by Hillegas.

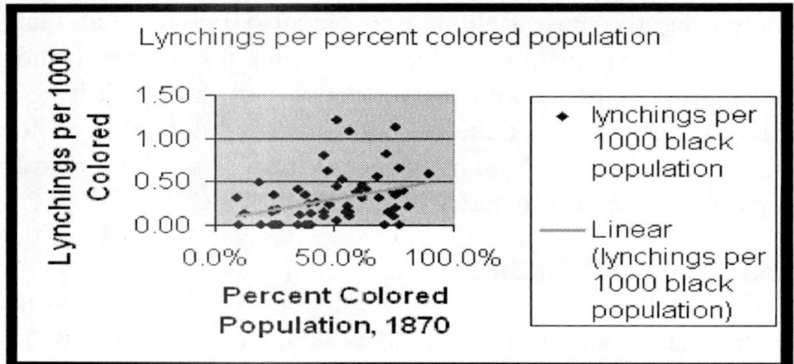

A similar calculation using the cube of the percent colored population as in Corzine, et al demonstrates a similar but more clearly seen correlation.

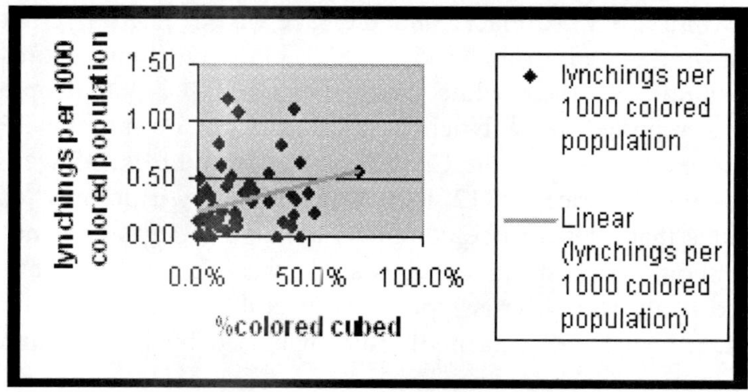

Initially, a comparison of lynching rates to claims presented to the Commission on Southern Claims seemed to indicate decrease in the rate of lynching compared to claims to the commission per county resident. However, this calculation was discarded as flawed, due to the law reserving claims only to Union loyalists. It is assumed, however dangerously, that union loyalists would be less likely to be lynchers. This could be a field for further study at another time.

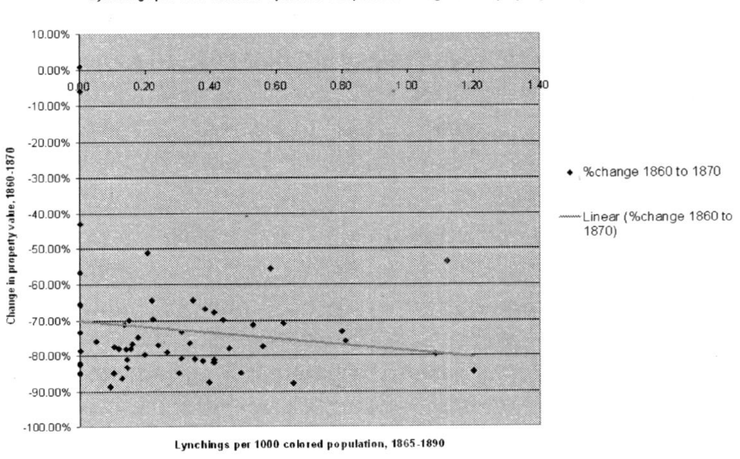

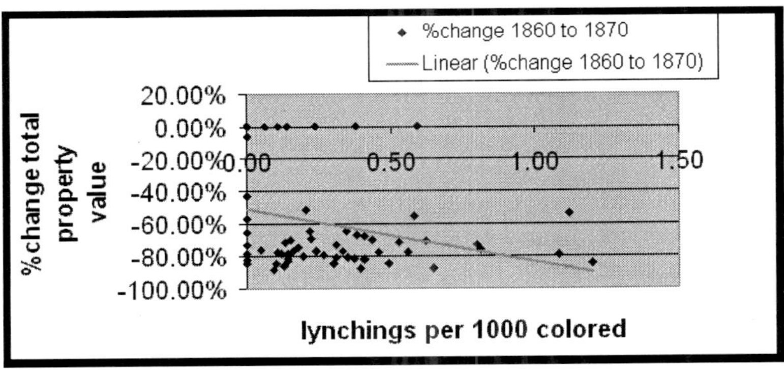

On further review, it was felt that a better indicator of war damages would be change in total property values from 1860 to 1870. Data from the 1860 and 1870 Censuses were used to determine the total value of real and personal property by county for the two years 1860 and 1870 and then calculate the percentage change over the decade of the war. (The negative of the 1860 Value minus the 1870 value divided by the 1860 value times 100.) The comparison of this number to the number of lynchings per 1000 colored population yielded a line showing that a greater negative change in total value of real and personal property by county over the course of the war correlated to an increase in the number of lynchings per 1000 colored population. This equates to a correlation, albeit not causation, between economic damage inflicted during the Civil War with an increased incidence of lynching in the years between the end of the war and Redemption.

Admittedly, this is a preliminary study and raises more questions than it provides answers. Any quantitative analysis of history must be meticulous in the use of numbers, and for a variety of reasons this study is not as precise as it could be. The purpose of this study is to function as an initial investigation into the possibility of economic influences on the incidence of lynching. It is not intended to forward any idea that lynching is not an expression of racist thuggery, no matter how it may be linked to economic conditions.

Like the course of the river for which it is named Mississippi's map has changed over the course of its history. County boundaries have changed frequently over the past century and a half. For example, DeSoto County was divided in 1873 to form DeSoto and what is now Tate County. Tate County also acquired land from Marshall County, thus an area that was once two counties is now three. Similar reboundarization occurred in Sunflower, Leflore, Bolivar and other counties. Drawing conclusions about occurrences described as happening in one Mississippi county or another during the 1800's should immediately raise questions about the temporal framework of the study, and what boundaries were used. Are the boundaries of the county listed as the site of any particular lynching the boundaries of today, or are they the boundaries at the time of the lynching? Further work to clarify this question would be desirable.

At this stage, it is most likely impossible to derive an exact figure for the number of extralegal executions in Mississippi during the 1800's. Any number quoted as a total for lynchings is an approximation at best. Problems with lynching statistics have been recognized for as long as lynching has been studied. The University Commission on Race Questions cited conflicting accounts for 1914. For that year, three different agencies, all of which have been cited as definitive at one time or another, quoted totals of 52, 54, and 72 lynchings. In any discussion of numbers of lynchings, the case of Rainey Poole must be remembered. After Poole's disappearance in 1971, the Sunflower River was dragged and two other bodies were found in addition to Poole's. Their families believed they had moved to Chicago. There is no doubt that over the years other people have "moved to Chicago" with no forwarding address.

Other areas for study regarding economic indicators and lynching abound. For example, an extension of Woofter's study of cotton land values, with allowances for inflation, into the Nineteenth Century might be useful. In view of the problems with the accuracy of the 1870 Census, a study of persistence of land ownership, similar to that of Wiener in Alabama, might yield more, if not better data relating to economic changes during and immediately after Reconstruction.

Lynching, a felony in some states in the U.S.A. is defined by some codes of law as "Any act of violence inflicted by a mob upon the body of another person which results in the death of the person," with a 'mob' being defined as "the assemblage of two or more persons, without color or authority of law, for the premeditated purpose and with the premeditated intent of committing an act of violence upon the person of another." Lynching in the second degree is defined as "Any act of violence inflicted by a mob upon the body of another person and from which death does not result." To sustain a conviction for lynching at least some evidence of premeditation must be produced, however "The common intent to do violence" may be formed before or during the assemblage."

The Dyer Anti-Lynching Bill was first introduced to United States Congress in 1918 by Congressman Leonidas Dyer of Missouri. The bill was passed by the House of Representatives in 1922 and in the same year given a favorable report by the Senate Committee; however, passage was halted by a Senate filibuster. The Dyer Bill has since influenced other anti-lynching legislation including the Costigan-Wagner Bill. The Dyer Anti-Lynching Bill as it appeared in 1922 stated: "To assure to persons within the jurisdiction of every State the equal protection of the laws, and to punish the crime of lynching... Be it enacted by the Senate and House of Representatives of the United States of America in Congress assembled, That the phrase "mob or riotous assemblage," when used in this act, shall mean an assemblage composed of three or more persons acting in concert for the purpose of depriving any person of his life without authority of law as a punishment for or to prevent the commission of some actual or supposed public offense."

In the United States, lynching is also a hate crime. Lynch mobs, which typically require a large number of participants, can be considered vigilante terrorists.

Lynching during the late nineteenth century in the United States, Great Britain and colonies, coincided with a period of high imperialism violence and religious inspired protest which denied people participation in white dominated society on the basis of race or gender after the Emancipation Act of 1833.

Pogroms against Jews in the early twentieth century in Russia and south-eastern Europe were another form of community policing, similar to the ethnic cleansing that characterized lynchings in the United States.

Lynching, as a form of punishment for presumed criminal offenses, performed by self-appointed commissions, mobs, or vigilantes without due process of law took place in the United States even before the American Civil War and after all over the nation from southern states to western frontier settlements. The term 'lynching' is believed to have originated during the American Revolution when Charles Lynch, a Virginia justice of the peace, ordered extralegal punishment for Tory acts. In the South, members of the abolitionist movement or other people opposing slavery were usually targets of lynch mob violence before the Civil War. After the war, lynching was a method of terrorism used to intimidate freed blacks who were voting and assuming political power. A study of vigilante justice during the period of 1868 to 1871 estimates that the Ku Klux Klan was involved in more than 400 lynchings. Blacks were lynched often because they were accused of crimes committed against whites, however, journalist Ida B. Wells showed in her investigations that many presumed crimes were exaggerated or didn't occur at all.

Mob violence became a tool for enforcing white supremacy and verged on systematic political terrorism. "The Ku Klux Klan, paramilitary groups, and other whites united by frustration and anger ruthlessly defended the interests of the Democratic party, the avowed party of white supremacy. The magnitude of extralegal violence during election campaigns reached epidemic proportions, leading the historian William Gillette to label it guerilla warfare."

During Reconstruction, the Ku Klux Klan and others used lynching as a means to control African Americans, force them to work for planters, and prevent them from voting.

White Republicans were often victims of lynching as well in the post-war period. Federal troops operating under the Civil Rights Act of 1871 largely broke up the Reconstruction-era Klan. By the end of Reconstruction in 1877, white southerners regained nearly total control of the region's governments and courts. In the late 19th century, Southern legislatures acted through constitutional changes and laws to effectively disfranchise African Americans through devices such as poll taxes or property requirements, and literacy and interpretation tests in which a registrar would judge a candidate's fitness.

Lynchings declined briefly, but the practice took hold again with a vengeance by the end of the 19th century. Tuskeegee Institute records of lynchings between the years 1880 and 1951 show 3437 African-American victims, as well as 1293 white victims, nearly all of whom were registered Republicans. The largest single lynching incident in America's history was the murder of 280 African Americans in Colfax, Louisiana in 1873 known as The Colfax Massacre.

The number of lynchings peaked at the end of the 19th century, but these kinds of murders continued into the twentieth century. African Americans resisted through protests, marches, writing of articles, rebuttals of so-called justifications of lynching, organizing women's groups against lynching, and organizing integrated groups against lynching. In addition African American playwrights produced fourteen anti-lynching plays from 1916-1935, ten of them by women. The frequency of lynching dropped in the 1930s. Most but not all lynchings ceased during the 1960s, but there were some dramatic cases of civil rights workers lynched in Mississippi.

After the 1915 release of the movie The Birth of a Nation, which glorified lynching and the Reconstruction-era Klan, the Klan re-formed and re-adopted lynching as a means to socially, economically, and politically terrorize and paralyze black populations. Victims were usually black men, and sometimes black women, often accused of assaulting or raping whites. Lynch Law declined sharply by the 1950s.

This memorial to the 1920 Duluth lynchings was described by its artist as attempting to "reinvest [the victims] with their unique personalities", to counteract the way the lynchings "depersonalized" them.

In *The Strange Career of Jim Crow,* the historian C. Vann Woodward wrote of the post—World War I period:

"The war-bred hopes of the Negro for first-class citizenship were quickly smashed in a reaction of violence that was probably unprecedented. Some twenty-five race riots were touched off in American cities during the first six months of 1919, months that John Hope Franklin called 'the greatest period of interracial strife the nation had ever witnessed.' Mobs took over cities for days at a time, flogging, burning, shooting, and torturing at will. When the Negroes showed a new disposition to fight and defend themselves, violence increased. Some of these atrocities occurred in the South—at Longview, Texas, for example, or at Tulsa, Oklahoma, at Elaine, Arkansas or Knoxville, Tennessee. But they were limited to no one section of the country. Many of them occurred in the North and the worst of all was in Chicago. During the first year following the war more than seventy Negroes were lynched, several of them veterans still in uniform."

The executions of 4,743 people who were lynched in the United States between 1882 and 1968 were not often publicized. It is likely that many more unrecorded lynchings occurred in this period. Lynching statistics were kept only for the 86 years between 1882 and 1968, and were based primarily on newspaper accounts. Yet the socio-political impact of lynchings could be significant. In 1901 the state of Colorado restored capital punishment, in response to an outbreak of lynchings in 1900. The state had abolished capital punishment only in 1897.

Most lynchings were inspired by unsolved crime, racism, and innuendo. 3,500 of its victims were African Americans. Lynchings took place in every state except four, but were concentrated in the Cotton Belt (Mississippi, Georgia, Alabama, Texas and Louisiana).

Members of mobs that participated in these public murders often took photographs of what they had done. Those photographs, distributed on postcards, were collected by James Allen, who has published them in book form and online, with written words and video to accompany the images.

Retaining incriminating evidence is not uncommon for sadistic criminals and in a study conducted by Robert R. Hazelwood, M.S. it was reported that of the sadistic criminals studied: "Forty percent of the men took and kept personal items belonging to their victims... which included... photographs... and some of the offenders referred to them as "trophies"."

Civil Rights and the Color of Law

The Fourth Amendment of the United States Constitution guarantees persons the right against unreasonable searches or seizures. Under the "color of law", a law enforcement official under certain circumstances is allowed to stop people and search them and retain their property if necessary. Abuse of this discretionary power is a violation of a person's civil rights. Unlawful detention or illegal confiscation of property are examples of such abuse. In deprivation of property, the color of law statute is violated by unlawfully obtaining or maintaining the property of another person. Fabricating evidence or conducting false arrest is a violation of a person's rights of unreasonable seizure and due process. The Fourteenth Amendment of the U.S. Constitution secures the right to due process. The Eighth Amendment prohibits the use of cruel and unusual punishment. These rights prohibit the use of force in an arrest or detention context which would amount to punishment or summary judgment and provide that a person accused of a crime is not subject to punishment without legal process and a trial. Title 18, U.S.C., Section 241 is the civil rights conspiracy statute which makes it unlawful for two or more persons to conspire to injure, oppress, threaten, or intimidate any person of any state, territory or district in the free exercise or enjoyment of any right or privilege secured to him/her by the Constitution or the laws of the United States, (or because of his/her having exercised the same) and further makes it unlawful for two or more persons to go in disguise on the highway or premises of another person with intent to prevent or hinder his or her free exercise or enjoyment of such rights. Depending upon the circumstances of the crime, and any resulting injury, the offense is punishable by a range of fines and/or imprisonment for any term of years up to life, or the death penalty.

LYNCHING IS A VIOLATION OF CIVIL RIGHTS

Europe

In Europe early examples of a similar phenomenon are found in the proceedings of the Vehmgerichte in medieval Germany, and of Lydford law, gibbet law or Halifax law in England and Cowper justice and Jeddart justice in Scotland.

In 1944, Wolfgang Rosterg, a German prisoner of war known to be unsympathetic to the Nazi regime in Germany, was lynched by Nazi fanatics in POW Camp 21 in Comrie, Scotland. After the end of the war, five of the perpetrators were hanged at Pentonville Prison—the largest multiple executions in 20th century Britain.

There are also some personal accounts of lynching in Budapest, Hungary, during the 1956 Hungarian Revolution against the occupying Soviets.

Mexico

On November 23, 2004, in the Tlahuac lynching, three Mexican undercover federal agents doing a narcotics investigation were lynched in the town of San Juan Ixtayopan (Mexico City) by an angry crowd who saw them taking photographs and mistakenly suspected they were trying to abduct children from a primary school. The policemen identified themselves immediately but were held and beaten for several hours before two of them were killed and set on fire. The whole incident was covered by the media almost from the beginning, including their pleas for help and their murder.

By the time police rescue units arrived, two of the policemen were reduced to charred corpses and the third was seriously injured. Authorities suspect the lynching was provoked by the persons being investigated.

Both local and federal authorities abandoned them to their fate, saying the town was too far away to even try to arrive in time and some officials stating they would provoke a massacre if they tried to rescue them from the mob.

Dominican Republic

Anti-black and anti-Haitian bias has long been a part of Dominican identity and culture. According to an Amnesty International report, lynchings of Haitians and black Dominicans have continued to occur as late as 2006.

South Africa

The practice of whipping and necklacing offenders and political opponents evolved in the 1980s during the apartheid era in South Africa. Residents of black townships lost confidence in the apartheid judicial system and formed "people's courts" that authorized whip lashings and deaths by necklacing. Necklacing is a term used to describe the torture and execution of victims by igniting a rubber, kerosene-filled, tire that has been forced around the victim's chest and arms. Necklacing was used to punish numerous victims, including children, who were alleged to be traitors to the black liberation movement as well as relatives and associates of the offenders. Of course sometimes the "people's courts" made mistakes, or used the system to punish those to whom leaders were opposed. There was tremendous controversy when the practice was endorsed by

Winnie Mandela, wife of the imprisoned Nelson Mandela and a senior member of the African National Congress.

India

Untold thousands of low-caste villagers have been lynched by upper-caste villagers throughout rural India. In November 2007, Kailash Bagri was lynched and burnt alive by upper-caste villagers in his village in Madhya Pradesh.. He was reportedly lynched by an upper-caste mob for shooing away cattle that belonged to an upper-caste villager with a stick. His body had been burnt so badly that his bones could not be recovered. Villagers were threatened not to tell anyone about the incident, but Mr. Bagri's son leaked the story to news sources.

In September 2007, a low-caste woman was burnt alive by upper-caste villagers in Uttar Pradesh because her son had eloped with a girl from a higher-caste. In August 2007, a policeman in Bihar beat and drowned two young low-caste girls in a river for stealing firewood from his orchard. A United Nations committee, equated violence against low-caste Hindus with racial discrimination and has questioned India's record on treatment of the socially marginalized

Lynching

Defined as an act of violence perpetrated for the purpose of punishment (usually torture and death) for an alleged crime carried out by an extralegal mob, lynching has a long history in the United States. Historians have traced its roots to seventeenth-century Ireland; the American Revolutionary War Colonel Charles Lynch, from whose name the term derives, was said to have indiscriminately meted out the punishment of flogging for Tory sympathizers. Lynch law, or mobrule, became part of the fabric of the United States; lynchings took place in every geographic section of the nation, and victims included African Americans, immigrants, and native-born whites. Alleged crimes varied, but most lynchings involved a perceived transgression of community values or a violation of societal honor codes.

During the antebellum period, lynch mobs across the country preyed upon individuals and groups deemed dangerous because they were political, religious, or racial "others." Abolitionists, Catholics, Mormons, Asian, Mexican, and European immigrants and African Americans all were targets. The pattern of mob violence and lynching changed after the Civil War. During the five decades between the end of Reconstruction and the New Deal, there were three specific transformations in the character of American lynching: increased numbers over all; increased likelihood that African Americans would fall victim to lynch mobs; and a concentration of lynchings in the South, particularly after 1886. The Tuskegee Institute started recording statistics on lynchings in 1882 (later, the Chicago Tribune and the National Association for the Advancement of Colored People [NAACP] also collected statistics). The first decade of those statistical findings best illustrates the transformation of lynching patterns. In 1882, 113 people were lynched, sixty-four whites and forty-nine African Americans. The year 1885 was the last during which more whites than African Americans were lynched, and 1892 witnessed the largest number of lynchings in U.S. history (230). From 1882 to 1903, there were approximately one to two hundred lynchings annually. Between 1882 and 1968, there were 4,742 recorded lynchings (3,445 of the victims were African American, or approximately seventy-five percent). During World War I

and the postwar red scare, race riots swept the country, wreaking havoc in Chicago, St. Louis, Tulsa, Omaha, Washington, D.C., and other cities. Lynchings decreased dramatically during the New Deal era, and the period between 1952 and 1954 was the longest during which no lynchings were recorded. But lynch mobs did not disappear completely. As civil rights workers stepped up their campaigns for desegregation and voting rights, they were beaten, killed, and tortured. Although some argue that race relations have improved, the tragedy of

American lynching has not been completely eradicated. The dragging death of James Byrd, in Texas, and the beating and crucifixion murder of Matthew Shepard in Wyoming have been called late twentieth-century lynchings.

There was, however, clearly a decline in lynching during the twentieth century, and this was a result of long and hard-fought battles of anti-lynching crusaders. In 1892, after three prominent Memphis businessmen were lynched, Ida B. Wells, the renowned journalist, began speaking out about the violence. She used Memphis newspaper, the Free Speech, to spread her outrage. She was soon joined by other prominent individuals and organizations. The founders of the NAACP in 1909 cited lynching as key to its formation and agenda. The organization was joined by the Association of Southern Women for the Prevention of Lynching in the 1930s. Wells's research did the most to destroy the myths about the causes of lynching, though it took decades for her findings to permeate mainstream American consciousness. In her pamphlet, "Southern Horrors: Lynch Law in All Its Phases," Wells argued that the majority of alleged rape charges were not only impossible to prove—that sexual liaisons between many black men and white women might have been consensual—but that rape was not even cited by mobs as the cause of lynching. Retribution for alleged homicide and assault were the most common reasons for the formation of lynch mobs. Legislation was a key goal of those who fought to punish the violence. Although many had tried to use the Fourteenth Amendment to prosecute lynchers, most efforts failed. In 1922, the House of Representatives passed the Dyer Anti-Lynching Bill, which had been sponsored by the NAACP. The bill died in the Senate, however, thanks to a filibuster by southern senators. Similar tactics were used to kill bills in 1937 and 1940. President Truman's Committee on Civil Rights recommended anti-lynching legislation but was ignored by Congress. Finally, in 1968, under the Civil Rights Act, the federal government could take action against mob violence and lynching.

Chapter 10

Animal Planet

Human social behaviour is a fascinating subject for observation. While socialization is not limited to humans, many animals move in herds and human socialization has the unique dimension of self-awareness. We become aware of what we are doing and we often lose spontaneity and get influenced by numerous factors. In particular, human social behaviour is influenced greatly by society's culture, as well as each person's self-image and world-image. Collective Behaviour is the way a group thinks, feels, or acts as a unit in response to an irrational process. Psychologist categorized crowd/group behaviour in two main theories: One, a crowd is less organized; they share a common approval/disapproval or similar emotion. Secondly, they share a common gesture, comments and stimulate similar behaviour and move the crowd. H.G Blumer categorized four types of crowds. One type of a crowd is a casual crowd which consists of curious people and they come together without

The study of individuals in groups and group behaviour has been a core of social psychology since its inception in the early 1900s. The definition of group that is used in most research is "people who are interdependent and have potential for mutual interaction.

Why People Come Together?

Sociology considers human social behaviour as something that involves much learning, and little of instincts. Overcrowding has been linked to bother physical and social disorders. The most prominent consequence of crowding or isolation for behaviours is violence. Modern sociology says that there is no instinctive basis for human social behaviour. An Emergent-Norm theory states that people come together for different reasons. The four types of mobs are:

- aggressive mob (physical violence),
- escape mob (inflict fear and pain),
- acquisitive mob (people who rush to acquire something when they believe that it has a short supply), and a

Expressive mob (people who are caught up in physical violence).

Mob, Individualistic or selfish thinking can identify mob behaviour. People displaying mob behaviour are tactical in that they think only for the moment and have virtually no strategic or long-term planning. In mob behaviour there is no leadership, which creates mob disorganization. When we think of street mobs, the first thing that comes to mind is violence, but actually violence is the product or outgrowth of disorganization, which happens because there is no effective leadership.

Birds and Mob Mentality

When songbirds perceive some sign of danger—a roosting owl, a hawk, a neighborhood cat—a group of them will often do something bizarre: fly toward the threat. When they reach the enemy, they will swoop down on it again and again, jeering and making a racket, which draws still more birds to the assault. The birds seldom actually touch their target (though reports from the field have it that some species can defecate or vomit on the predator with "amazing accuracy"). The barrage simply continues until the intruder sulks away. Scientists call this behaviour "mobbing."

Birds mob for a couple of reasons. One of them is educational: Youngsters learn whom to mob, and whom to fear, by watching others do it. But the more immediate purpose of mobbing is to drive the predator away—or, in the words of the eminent Austrian ethnologist Konrad Lorenz, to make "the enemy's life a burden."

White Collar Mobbing

In the early 1980s, Heinz Leymann, a German psychologist working in Sweden, was conducting clinical studies of workers who had encountered violence on the job. At the time, plenty of research had already been done on the "mental insufficiency" experienced by soldiers after wartime and the survivors of major industrial disasters. So Leymann set out to study some of the less obvious cases of post-traumatic stress. He carried out longitudinal studies of Stockholm subway drivers who had accidentally run over people with their trains. He studied the psychological effects of robberies on bank tellers. But he stumbled upon an even less obvious group that showed the most surprisingly acute measures of stress. These were people whose colleagues had ganged up on them at work. Inspired by Lorenz's writings on animal mobbing, Leymann coined the term "workplace mobbing" to name the phenomenon. He defined it as "an impassioned, collective campaign by co-workers to exclude, punish, and humiliate a targeted worker."

Leymann drew up a list of 45 mobbing indicators. It amounted to an impressive catalog of bureaucratic nastiness: "You are interrupted constantly"; "you are isolated in a room far from others"; "management gives you no possibility to communicate"; "you are given meaningless work tasks"; "you are given dangerous work tasks"; "you are treated as if you are mentally ill." Though Leymann is relatively unknown in North America, his research on mobbing has been remarkably influential in Europe. Das mobbing is a household term in Germany. France has even passed anti-mobbing laws.

Max Weber, a founding father of modern sociology, saw bureaucracy as the living embodiment of cool, procedural rationality. In Mr. Westhues's view, mobbing is a pathological undercurrent of irrationality in bureaucracies—a crabby ghost in the machine.

With his mobbing research, Mr. Westhues joins a tradition of thinkers who present an account of some deep-seated impulse as a plea for pluralism and restraint. And while he says it is possible to take mobbing seriously without believing we all have those herd instincts that belief helps.

Why do Mobs Behave in Such Extreme Ways?

Groups have incredible effects on individuals' behaviours, and have been an area of interest in social psychology for years. Psychologists have found that group behaviour tends to be more extreme than the typical behaviour of its individual members. This phenomenon is most clearly seen in the behaviour of mobs. A mob is one of the most influential (and overlooked) forces in changing people's behaviour. Social Psychologists attribute this effect to a process of de-individuation, defined as the loosening of normal constraints on behaviour when people are in a crowd, leading to an increase in impulsive and deviant acts.

Groups encourage a sense of anonymity among its members, and it is this anonymity that results in "mob psychology" and other anti-social behaviours. When people think they are anonymous, they will behave in anti-social ways because they so not believe they can be singled out among the crowd and be evaluated. Groups also encourage a diffusion of responsibility for actions taken. Thus, if an individual acts in an anti-social manner while in a group, it is the group's fault as well as his. This leads to an overall weakening of social influences and self-consciousness. Social norms no longer apply to members of the group, but rather, the group creates its own set of norms to which every member adheres. Inevitably, the result is antisocial behaviour on the part of the individual and the group.

The presence of a group influence has a large impact on individual behaviours. A person may find himself in a totally different psychological state than he usually resides. This is mob psychology. Social norms no longer have any effect on individual behaviour and there is no longer any fear of evaluation for one's actions. Increased anonymity, diffusion of responsibility, and the increased energy that results from the existence of a group lead to a weakened self-consciousness, and encourage individuals to behave in ways that would not belong in normal social environments.

Group Polarization

In groups, people tend to be more extreme in their decisions.

Risky Shift Phenomenon

When people are in groups, they make decision about risk differently from when they are alone. In the group, they are likely to make riskier decisions, as the shared risk makes the individual risk less.

They also may not want to let their compatriots down, and hence be risk-averse (this is sometimes called cautious shift). The overall tendency towards a shift in risk perception is also sometimes called choice shift.

There are a number of reasons as to why this might happen. Theories have included:

Wallach, Kogan, and Bem (1964) proposed that greater risks are chosen due to a diffusion of responsibility, where emotional bonds decrease anxieties and risk is perceived as shared.

Collins and Guetzkow (1964) suggested that high risk-takers are more confident and hence may persuade others to take greater risks.

Brown (1965) indicates that social status in groups is often associated with risk-taking, leading people to avoid a low risk position.

Bateson (1966) suggests that as people pay attention to a possible action, they become more familiar and comfortable with it and hence perceive less risk.

Group polarization has been used to explain the decision-making of a jury, particularly when considering punitive damages in a civil trial. Studies have shown that after deliberating together, mock jury members often decided on punitive damage awards that were larger or smaller than the amount any individual juror had favored prior to deliberation. The studies indicated that when the jurors favored a relatively low award, discussion would lead to an even more lenient result, while if the jury was inclined to impose a stiff penalty, discussion would make it even harsher.

Persuasive Arguments Theory

Before meeting in a group, members of the group will develop arguments to support their positions. To sway others, the arguments will tend to be more extreme. In the end, one argument will win and the group will find itself supporting an extreme decision.

Groupthink

Groupthink is a concept that was identified by Irving Janis9 that refers to faulty decision-making in a group. Groups experiencing groupthink do not consider all alternatives and they desire unanimity at the expense of quality decisions.

Conditions	Groupthink occurs when groups are highly cohesive and when they are under considerable pressure to make a quality decision.

(*Contd.*)

Negative outcomes	Some negative outcomes of groupthink include: • Examining few alternatives • Not being critical of each other's ideas • Not examining early alternatives • Not seeking expert opinion • Being highly selective in gathering information • Not having contingency plans
Symptoms	Some symptoms of groupthink are: • Having an illusion of invulnerability • Rationalizing poor decisions • Believing in the group's morality • Sharing stereotypes which guide the decision • Exercising direct pressure on others • Not expressing your true feelings • Maintaining an illusion of unanimity • Using mindguards to protect the group from negative information

Self-Fulfilling Prophecy

In everything we do or fail to do, we communicate attitudes and values that others take as cues for their own behaviour and attitudes. These communicated attitudes and expectations act as self-fulfilling prophecies. The theory of the self-fulfilling prophecy holds that people tend to do what is expected of them and that even a false expectation can evoke behaviour that makes it seem true. Our belief that something will happen can actually make it happen.

Self-Concept

Once we have developed a particular image of ourselves—a particular self-concept—we all go to great efforts to maintain it. We even distort information to maintain our self-image. We see things not as they are but as we think they are. Individuals tend to avoid information contrary to their beliefs and to seek information supporting their views.

The work we do defines and confirms our social roles as well as our self-concept. Each person, of course, has many roles, and the rules for each are carefully defined—for parent, spouse, friend, enemy, teacher, doctor, housewife, and so forth. Role definitions have many advantages, but they also present many problems, especially when role requirements are ambiguous or contradictory. An individual may imperceptibly become the kind of person the situation requires him or her to be, even at the expense of his or her scruples, values, or convictions.

But the reverse also is true—our attitudes and personality can affect our roles. For example, if I dislike controversy, I am not likely to become a soldier or a lawyer.

Work is crucially important in this context because it can shape personality. An individual tends to become the kind of person the situation demands. When a worker becomes a middle manager, he or she finds his or her attitude toward top supervisors changing just as a former supervisor finds his or her attitude toward the union changing when he or she becomes a union shop steward.

In other words, while attitudes can affect behaviour, it also is true that behaviour can affect attitudes, an idea summed up in the maxim that it is easier to act your way into a new way of thinking than it is to think your way into a new way of acting!

Motivation

The most common view of motivation is that human beings are rational animals motivated by money and other material rewards. And for many people in many situations, money is important. However, some people place greater value on social approval, prestige, and status than on money.

This view of man as a social animal emphasizes that man is governed more by the informal organization's logic of sentiments than by the formal organization's logic of efficiency. More recently, behavioural scientists have found that high employee morale does not necessarily result in greater productivity and that man's motivations are vastly more complex than can be explained in economic or social terms alone. Many theorists and managers now believe that the psychological contract implies that effort be exchanged not only for money and social contact but for self-esteem, autonomy, and self-actualization.

Animal Planet

In a democratic country like ours where there is a judicial system in place what makes people take the law in their hands when it comes to meting out justice; Medieval justice preference to Modern Justice. What is alarming is that these instances take place even in the presence of the police.

In India, mobs are above the law. The events in Rajasthan in the last few days are an illustration of this. The losses to business because of the protests by the Gujjars and their clashes with the Meenas are estimated to run in the hundreds of crores

Mob violence is often not controlled even when it can be, which is not something you'll see in the UK or the US. How often have police in India been known to stand by and watch as rioters damage property and/or people? They do this mostly because they know that the violence they are witnessing is not a

mere law-and-order issue, but a political one. It is outside their domain.

Any mob activity that has political sanction has, by default, the implicit support of the law-and-order machinery. This applies to bandhs, to morchas, to strikes and even to riots, as we saw in Delhi in 1984 and Gujarat in 2002. And because the polity is so fractured and votebank politics is commonplace, many relatively small groups—such as the Gujjars—can disrupt normal life and get away with it.

While the police is biased towards the powerful, the legal system is also dysfunctional. Even if someone gets arrested for rioting—it has been known to happen, though always at the bottom of the food chain—do you seriously expect him to be brought to justice? The fellow will get bail, the case will drag on for years, the cops will be too incompetent to file a proper chargesheet and witnesses will change their tune. In the end, justice will not be done.

Nothing insulates mob violence in India such as the excuse of religion. Forget religious riots—have you ever tried walking the streets of Mumbai during Ganpati, when drunk young men clog the streets, dancing and throwing colour with abandon? Anything that is done in India under the guise of religion is immune to the law.

Festivals in India enable mob misbehaviour, and the way they are celebrated in modern times virtually gives social sanction for hooliganism. This applies even to a relatively non-religious festival like Holi, which is no longer a wholesome celebration of spring but an excuse to harass women (and even men, sometimes) whom one doesn't know. In theory our religions preach love but in practice they perpetuate hatred and suspicion. Our collective national conscious is questionable.

Mahatma Gandhi's ways of non-violence perhaps gave rise to a population that was devoid of any fighting spirit. We became used to accepting violence, first from the British and then from our own oppressors. Violence is an injustice, and when you accept injustice than you lose sense of justice. We turn barbaric when we face a submissive opponent and we become helpless (peace-loving) victims when a strong opponent attacks us, whether from within the country or from outside.

Now, mobs are a problem across the world. Sports-related mob violence takes place in most of the developed countries, and earlier this week around 1000 people were injured at protests at the G8 summit at Rostock. But mostly, police struggle to stop such violence because of logistical issues. Countries across the world recruit police keeping relatively normal times in mind, and find themselves over-stretched when riots take place.

"Softened" Culprit

Mob justice is a common phenomenon across the country in which a suspect, if caught by the local populace, is often "softened" before being handed to the police. The police further torture the person to extract a confession, and the entire investigation of the case is based upon this forced confession. Cases brought to court based on evidence gathered following a forced confession by torture stand little chance of succeeding during a trial, and thus, the result is an acquittal of the accused; given the socio-economic conditions in India, the chance of an acquitted person being caught while committing yet another crime is very high. Additionally, there is an enormous delay, often for periods of six to seven years or even a decade, for the courts to complete a trial. The net result is the loss of the perception of justice in the mind of the public. Consequently, in this context, it is natural at this juncture for the public to take the law into their own hands and render instant justice upon anyone whom they suspect of a crime.

Mob justice continues to rule Bihar. Men are lynched by villagers in Vaishali on suspicion they were robbers. The men were spotted by a villager who raised an alarm. Within minutes a mob of over 200 lynched the men with sticks, clubs and stones. Police arrived well after the incident. Locals claim that thefts have been on the rise in the area and the request for deploying of police fell on deaf ears. Police had not been taking complaints of robbery by villagers seriously enough. Police personnel agree that robberies could be the reason why the villagers decided to take matters into their hands to deliver instant justice. Bihar C.M. Nitesh Kumar has proposed to start awareness campaign against mob fury. Educating the masses is the need of the hour. The most disturbing characteristic of mob behaviour is the ability of the mob to dominate public opinion.

P.M. Manmohan Singh in one of his speeches made his views on mob justice very clear. He stated some of these reactions could be the result of personal frustration, but some of them also arose out of dissatisfaction over functioning of the law enforcement agencies and justice system. The police force should be able to reach out to citizens and win their confidence and affection. Police forces needed to do their job in a manner that basics of law enforcement were catered to in a fair, humane, honest, and competent manner. Top cops should introspect and see they were addressing people's concerns and meeting their expectations. He further added that maintenance of law and order on matters which directly impinge citizenry is an important issue which often gets neglected.

The Supreme Court said people started thinking that justice won't be done in courts due to delays in proceedings. It is the result of the erosion of their faith in courts' capability to render speedy justice. People of India are simply disgusted with the state of affairs and are losing faith in the judiciary. This is indeed an alarming state of affairs and concerned authorities should act to do the needful urgently before the situation goes out of control. CJI G. Balakrishnan says it is not so much the judiciary's fault as it is the executive's.

Although politicians (and the media) tend to regard mob justice as collective hysteria and moral failure, quite clearly it is intimately connected with public frustration over the nation's collapsing law, order and justice systems. India has a mere 1,000 policemen per million people and in most of the 485 districts of rural India; the writ of the police doesn't run after 6 p.m. The Indian legal system characterized by archaic procedures and pervasive corruption has accumulated a backlog of over 30 million cases. Little wonder with public confidence in the law, order and justice systems at an all-time low, people are resorting to vigilantism and mob justice.

Curiously the ground reality that India has fewer than 13 judges per million people, whereas the UK has 50, Canada 75 and the US 107, doesn't seem to trouble the consciences of politicians or the public. And even the 13,000 judges countrywide grudgingly employed by government are provided abysmal infrastructure and support services. Government expenditure on the legal system aggregates a mere 0.42 percent of GDP annually cf. 4.3 percent in the UK.

Sometimes vigilantism is wrongly equated with self-defense. Vigilante behaviour is premeditative while self-defense is spontaneous. Vigilantes do not care for the police to finish their investigation and courts to punish the offenders. They seek swift and sure punishment. Lynch mobs, as psychologists point out, arm themselves with a sense of retributive righteousness. They mean to exert social control by exemplary doses of terror on the notion that the violence is the only language that the victims understand.

Mobs go unruly at the sight of T.V. cameras. Do the media give such incidents undue hype? It is those folk who crave for ten minutes of fame on visual media are always at the forefront and who try to act as the moral police. Just how and when mob fury turns ugly has been there for all to see. T.V. channels thrive on cheap publicity and such incidents only serve as fodder. Not much seems to have changed since past times. Physical violence committed upon a person is equally traumatic for the witness as well as the victim. Psychological trauma, if mapped on a scale from one to 10 and if the victim of physical violence suffers mental trauma at point 10, the witness to the incident, including the assaulter, suffers from metal trauma at point nine.

For both categories of people—the victim and the witnesses—a single incident is a traumatic experience whose effects last throughout their lifetime. This is because the average human mind is not equipped to withstand a high degree of psychological violence. Consequently, in incidents of mob justice, the number of people who are exposed to severe psychological trauma is very high. If not over-generalizing or exaggerating, an increase in mob justice in any country means there are more people suffering from psychological trauma in that country. Given the high number of incidents of mob justice in India, hundreds of Indians today suffer from psychological trauma associated with partaking in the incident or by witnessing it.

What we see today could merely be revival of a tradition long buried under the anglicized annals of penal codes and archives of dusty, musty case studies. What has perhaps changed is the role media has played in popularizing our vigilante force

People have lost faith in the 'system'-an amorphous amalgam of politician, the police, the judiciary, the bureaucracy, etc. and vent their frustrations in outbursts of mob frenzy, spurred on by a sensation hungry media that highlights such incidents.

Rising vigilantism and recourse to rough and ready mob justice is also fed by the conspicuous failure of state governments to arrest and file charges against vigilante groups. In none of the horrific incidents of mob violence, have arrests been made by the police. Such inaction and condo nation of vigilantism is tantamount to tacit approval of on-the-spot mob justice.

However elimination of lynch justice and establishing the rule of law requires more than mere moral exhortation. Criminal—perhaps deliberate—neglect of law and order and judicial infrastructure are issues which need to be urgently addressed and remedied. If not, dispensation of rough-n-ready mob justice will become the rule rather than exception in shining, fast-track India.

Mob rule represents a far graver danger than that of sporadic violence; it questions the very existence of the state as a whole. In this sense mob violence is as subversive of the state as a campaign of terrorism. When the state monopoly fails private players step up to fill the gap. These private players include rampaging mobs and armed insurgents. The brick and the bullet and the flaming torch replace the rule of law and disorder.

The temptation to take law in one's own hands is much greater when people believe that they can get away playing vigilantes. It is necessary for the police and political authorities to deal firmly with vigilantism, making clear that this form of criminal activity will be put down firmly. Do-it-yourself justice represents a serious threat to democracy and to the rule of law.

If an alarming number of incidents of mob justice are reported from a particular region or country, it strongly suggests that there is something terribly wrong in the societal framework and its justice delivery mechanisms. People feel that the police service is also not helping them at all because they take bribes, and some of the thieves know people in the police service, so it becomes useless of you to take such an alleged thief to them. Moreover our system is such that one needs to really prove beyond reasonable doubt that a fellow is guilty before prosecution takes place. For the police protection issue, it can never be enough because the ratio of police officers to citizens is very few. Security wise, the police is not doing much because of logistics and lack of human personnel? although they doing what they can.

In the UK Naomi Campbell [the supermodel] beat up her maidservant and court asked her to go to do some community service, and I think we should be doing that in our system so that the issue of instant justice will be reduced

It is an inherent part of human nature to instantaneously decide what is good and evil. However, it is not by nature a primordial human trait to decide what punishment is just for a crime and what is not. It is because of this human shortcoming and because of a number of other reasons, like maintaining order, that human society, irrespective of race, ethnicity and region, has evolved various forms of mechanisms for rendering justice throughout history.

Taking law unto one's own hand can only lead to more mess which is visible. A crime has to be established through an investigative process and punishment has to be decided only through a designated authority under the due process of law. It has to be free of passion and commensurate with the nature of crime. A Kangaroo court or a mob's decision to lynch, blind or drag some one after tying to steal a bike is damaging.

People wonder why the whole thing is branded as "instance justice." If really it is instant justice, it should have some kind of justice element? but not when someone who is suspected as a thief is lynched.

sociology has explained mob actions? that is an action which people take as a result of being part of a group. It only takes one person in a crowd around a suspected criminal to call for lynching and others join in.

The police must also be fast in training, because people get frustrated seeing criminals free on the street after sending them to the police station, and this motivates people to beat up alleged thieves. Culprits should be brought to book. Let's allow the law to take it's course.

When an offense is alleged against a person, irrespective of time and region, there were, and are, mechanisms that decided the punishment, however just or unjust the punishment may be. The societies that practiced mob justice lacked order, and the perception of justice was reduced to a very minimal level of an eye for an eye. It appears that India is unfortunately headed toward turning the whole of India blind.

We have to use media constructively to highlight the cases of ineptness and shirking away of responsibility by authorities and agencies meant for keeping order. Usurping the role of investigative and judicial agencies by mobs is certainly not a renaissance. It is a recipe for anarchy and must be resisted with.

Such vigilante justice, when the police fails to do its due, seems justified on the surface. But the manner in which it is carried out, and the sardonic spin given to such incidents by the mockery that is Indian media today stands out merely as comic relief in our already stress-laden, sorry lives.

Police administration is there to take care of common citizen in each country but a majority of officers have become corrupt and they do nothing to save people from criminals. In that case self justice to save our lives from criminals at times results in mob justice.

People then don't talk about ethics because when the administration and government cannot provide security, people get no option but to take law in their hands to save them and their family members from activities of unsocial elements.

Index